DOCUMENTS AND DESCRIPTIONS IN
EUROPEAN HISTORY 1815–1939

DOCUMENTS AND DESCRIPTIONS IN EUROPEAN HISTORY
1815–1939

Selected and edited

by

R. W. BREACH, B.A.

Head of the History Department,
Larkfield Grammar School, Chepstow

OXFORD UNIVERSITY PRESS

1964

Oxford University Press, Amen House, London E.C.4

GLASGOW NEW YORK TORONTO MELBOURNE WELLINGTON
BOMBAY CALCUTTA MADRAS KARACHI LAHORE DACCA
CAPE TOWN SALISBURY NAIROBI IBADAN ACCRA
KUALA LUMPUR HONG KONG

*Printed in Great Britain by Richard Clay and Company, Ltd.,
Bungay, Suffolk*

Contents

CONTENTS

CONTENTS

CONTENTS

CONTENTS

CONTENTS

Introduction

The purpose of this book is to provide a modest collection of extracts from original sources, in English, to illustrate the period 1815–1939 in European history. The book is intended mainly for the upper forms of Secondary Schools, is confined to the obviously significant events, and should present no difficulties of understanding or interpretation to anyone with an outline knowledge of the period. Each pupil should have a copy for normal class use.

The material used could have been collected in various sections, as for instance, the rebellions of 1848, but it seemed the book would be easier to use if the extracts were collected under national headings, with an extra section for material which did not fit easily into these.

Most of the extracts can be used as a basis for classroom discussion or for comment prepared at home, and one of the besetting faults of school history, the passive noting and absorption of second-hand material, to some extent avoided.

The book contains a balance of the two elements: important documents that helped to make the history, and descriptions of that history by eye-witnesses. There is no section on British or American history, for lack of space, but I have tried to indicate how British and American attitudes influenced events.

In the interests of economy, and relevance for the class of readers I have in mind, I have often omitted material, but the following rules have been observed.

INTRODUCTION

1. I have used square brackets [ ] to show comment, explanation, or summary of intervening material made by the editor.

2. Asterisks * * * show where whole paragraphs, sections, or clauses of treaties have been left out.

3. Dots . . . indicate the omission of sentences in paragraphs.

4. In some cases material is described as condensed. This is applied to descriptive material, where sentences have been run together, etc.

I have made every effort to avoid any change in the meaning. The sceptic can look up the original for himself.

January 1964   R.W.B.

Acknowledgements

The editor and publishers wish to thank the following publishers, authors, and translators for permission to use copyright material:

Messrs. Ginn & Co. (Boston) for extracts from Robinson and Beard, *Readings in Modern European History*, vol. II (1, 2a, 3, 4, 5a, 6a, 8, 9, 10, 11b, 12a, 12b, 17, 18, 19a, 20, 22, 27, 28, 32, 35, 36, 37a, 37b, 37c, 38, 42b, 44a, 44b, 44c, 49)

Oxford University Press for extracts from H. W. V. Temperley *A History of the Peace Conference of Paris*, vol. III (published under the auspices of the Royal Institute of International Affairs) (53); V. Serge, *Memoirs of a Revolutionary* (34a); I. Deutscher, *Stalin* (34c); N. N. Sukhanov, *The Russian Revolution* (tr. Joel Carmichael) (33b); Leo Tolstoy, *What Then Must We Do* (tr. Aylmer Maude) (30); *Hitler's Speeches* 1922–39, tr. N. H. Baynes (published under the auspices of the Royal Institute of International Affairs) (15b, 15c, 15d); R. W. Mowat, *Select Treaties and Documents* (41b, 6d, 21)

Keesings Publications Ltd. for material from *Keesings Contemporary Archives* (7d, 7e, 39b, 55)

Routledge & Kegan Paul Ltd. for an extract from M. Dobb, *Soviet Economic Development since 1917* (34b)

John Murray (Publishers) Ltd. for an extract from Leo Deutsch, *Sixteen Years in Siberia* (31)

Cambridge University Press for extracts from R. W.

ACKNOWLEDGEMENTS

Seton-Watson, *Masaryk in England* (43), and A. W. Ward and C. P. Gooch, *The Cambridge History of British Foreign Policy* (13b)

Chatto & Windus Ltd. for 'Dulce et Decorum Est', from *The Poems of Wilfred Owen* (50b)

Lawrence & Wishart Ltd. for extracts from Lenin, *Towards the Seizure of Power*, Book I (33) and *The Communist Manifesto*, tr. Eden and Cedar Paul (47)

Methuen & Co. Ltd. for extracts from H. Butterfield, *Select Historical Documents*, vol. III (2b, 16, 41a, 42a, 45)

Hodder & Stoughton Ltd. for an extract from N. Henderson, *Failure of a Mission* (15g)

Mr. F. Jellinek for an extract from *The Paris Commune of 1871* (5)

Constable & Co. Ltd. and Sir Harold Nicolson for an extract from *Peacemaking 1919* (52)

The Catholic University of America for an extract from Agnes Murphy, *The Ideology of French Imperialism* (6b)

Cassell & Co. Ltd. for extracts from W. S. Churchill, *The Second World War* (15f, 39c), and van Bulow, *Imperial Germany*, tr. M. A. Lewenz (13a)

Macmillan & Co. Ltd. for extracts from *Gustav Stresemann, His Diaries, Letters and Papers*, tr. Eric Sutton (14), and (with the Trustees of the Estate of the late Lord Keynes) J. M. Keynes, *Essays in Biography* (7a)

Rupert Hart-Davis Ltd. for an extract from Guy Chapman, *The Dreyfus Case* (6c)

Oswald Wolff (Publishers) Ltd. for an extract from Gerhard Ritter, *The Schlieffen Plan* (13c)

The Hutchinson Publishing Group for an extract from Adolf Hitler, *Mein Kampf*, tr. James Murphy (15a)

Stanford University Press and the Trustees of the Leland

ACKNOWLEDGEMENTS

Stanford Junior University, for extracts from James H. Bunyan and H. H. Fisher, *The Bolshevik Revolution 1917–1918* (Copyright 1934 renewed 1962 by James H. Bunyan and H. H. Fisher) (33d, 33e)

Sidgwick & Jackson Ltd. for 'The Dead' from *The Collected Poems of Rupert Brooke* (50a)

The Times Publishing Co. Ltd. for material from *The Times* (7b, 15e, 23, 25, 26, 39a, 40b, 44d, 54)

Dr. Hanz Schwarzmantel Ph.D. for translations from Bismarck's *Gedanken*

While every effort has been made to trace the owners of all copyright material, in a few cases this has proved impossible. In the event of this book reaching them, the publishers would be glad if they would communicate with them, so that they may acknowledge their obligation in any future edition.

France

1. The Charter of 1814

This Charter was first issued by King Louis XVIII, the Bourbon restored by the Allies, in 1814, between Napoleon's retirement to Elba and his return, 'the 100 days'. In form it is a grant made by the grace of the divinely appointed monarch.

Source: Tripier, *Constitutions qui ont régi la France* (1879), pp. 229 ff., in Robinson and Beard, *Readings in Modern European History* II, 2–5.

Louis, by the grace of God king of France and Navarre, to all those to whom these presents come, salutation:

Divine Providence, in recalling us to our estates after a long absence, has imposed grave responsibilities upon us. Peace was the first necessity of our subjects, and with this we have unceasingly occupied ourselves. That peace so essential to France and to the rest of Europe has been signed.

A constitutional charter was demanded by the existing condition of the kingdom; we promised this and now publish it. We have taken into consideration the fact that, although the whole authority in France resides in the person of the king, our predecessors have not hesitated to modify the exercise of this in accordance with the different needs of the times. . . .

We, like the kings our predecessors, have had to consider the effects of the ever-increasing progress of knowledge, the new relations which this progress has introduced into society, the direction given to the public mind during half a century, and the serious troubles resulting therefrom.

B   I

We have perceived that the wish of our subjects for a constitutional charter was the expression of a real need; but in yielding to this wish we have taken every precaution that this charter should be worthy of us and of the people whom we are proud to rule. Able men taken from the highest official bodies of the State were added to the commissioners of our council to elaborate this important work.

*　　*　　*

Confident in our intentions, strong in our conscience, we engage ourselves, before the assembly which listens to us, to be faithful to this constitutional charter; with the intention, moreover, of swearing to maintain it with added solemnity before the altars of Him who weighs in the same balance kings and nations.

For these reasons we have voluntarily, and by the free exercise of our royal authority, granted and do grant, concede, and accord, as well for us as for our successors forever, the Constitutional Charter as follows:

Public Rights of the French

Article 1. All Frenchmen are equal before the law, whatever may be their title or rank.

2. They contribute without distinction to the impositions of the State in proportion to their fortune.

3. They are all equally eligible for civil and military positions.

4. Their personal liberty is likewise guaranteed; no one can be prosecuted or arrested except in the cases and in the manner prescribed by law.

5. All may with equal liberty make profession of their religion and enjoy the same protection for their worship.

6. Nevertheless the Roman Catholic and apostolic religion is the religion of the State.

7. The ministers of the Roman Catholic and apostolic religion, and those of other Christian forms of worship only, shall receive subsidies from the royal treasury.

8. All Frenchmen have the right to publish and cause their opinions to be printed, if they conform to the laws designed to check the abuse of this liberty.

9. All property is inviolable; that known as national property forms no exception, since the law recognizes no difference between that and other property.

10. The State may demand the surrender of property in the interest of the public when this is legally certified, but only with previous indemnification.

11. All investigation of opinions expressed or of votes cast previous to the Restoration is prohibited; oblivion of these is imposed upon the courts and upon citizens alike.

12. Conscription is abolished; the method of recruiting both for the army and the navy shall be determined by law.

Form of the Government of the King

13. The person of the king is inviolable and sacred; his ministers are responsible. In the king alone is vested the executive power.

14. The king is the supreme head of the State; he has command of the land and naval forces, declares war, concludes treaties of peace, alliance, and commerce, appoints all the officials of the public administration, and issues the regulations and ordinances necessary for the execution of the laws and the safety of the State.

15. The legislative power is exercised jointly by the king, the Chamber of Peers, and the Chamber of Deputies of the departments.

16. The right of initiating legislation belongs to the king.

17. Proposed laws are submitted, at the option of the

king, either to the Chamber of Peers or to the Chamber of Deputies, except laws for raising taxes, which must be submitted to the Chamber of Deputies first.

18. Every law must be discussed and passed freely by a majority of each of the two houses.

19. The chambers have the right to petition the king to submit a law relating to any subject and to indicate what they deem the law should contain. . . .

[There are further sections on the two Chambers, the Judges, etc.]

2. The Revolution of July 1830

(a) Charles X's Press Law

The following Ordinance against the Press, of 25 July, was one of three which precipitated the Revolution.

Source: Duvergier, *Collection complète des lois, décrets*, etc., (1824) XXX, 74–78, in Robinson and Beard, pp. 11–12.

On the report of our Council of Ministers, we have ordained and ordain as follows:

Article 1. The liberty of the periodical press is suspended.

2. The provisions of articles 1, 2, and 9 of the first section of the law of the 21st of October, 1814, are again put in force, in consequence of which no journal, or periodical, or semi-periodical work, regardless of the character of the matters therein treated, established, or about to be established, shall appear either in Paris or in the departments, except by virtue of an authorization first obtained from us by the authors and the printer respectively. This authorization shall be renewed every three months. It may also be revoked.

* * *

4. Newspapers and writings published in contravention of article 2 shall be immediately seized. The presses and types used in the printing of them shall be placed in a public warehouse under seals, or rendered unfit for use.

* * *

Given at Chateau St. Cloud, the 25th of July, of the year of grace 1830, and the sixth of our reign.

(Signed) Charles

(b) Orleanist poster of 30 July 1830

This poster expresses the views of the moderates led by Thiers.

Source: Lavisse, *Histoire de la France Contemporaine*, Vol. IV, p. 378 (1920–22), in H. Butterfield, *Select Historical Documents*, III, 114.

Charles X must not be allowed in Paris again: he has shed the blood of the people.

A Republic would expose us to terrible dissension; it would embroil us with Europe.

The Duke of Orleans is a prince devoted to the cause of the Revolution.

The Duke of Orleans has never fought against us.

The Duke of Orleans was at Jemappes.

The Duke of Orleans has worn the republican colours under fire; he alone can wear them now; we do not want any other colours.

The Duke of Orleans has made a statement; he accepts the Charter as we have always wanted it to be accepted.

It is from the French people that he will hold his crown.

3. The Revolution of 1848

These two documents show clearly the emotions surrounding the Revolution and the aims of the new government.

(a) Proclamation of the 2nd Republic, 26 February 1848

Source: Duvergier, XLVIII, 49, in Robinson and Beard, pp. 80–81.

In the name of the French people:

Citizens; royalty, under whatever form, is abolished; no more legitimism, no more Bonapartism, no regency.

The provisional government has taken all the measures necessary to render impossible the return of the former dynasty or the advent of a new dynasty.

The republic is proclaimed.

The people are united.

All the forts which surround the capital are ours.

The brave garrison of Vincennes is a garrison of brothers.

Let us retain that old republican flag whose three colours made with our fathers the circuit of the globe.

Let us show that this symbol of equality, of liberty, and of fraternity is at the same time the symbol of order,—of order the more real, the more durable, since justice is its foundation and the whole people its instrument.

The people have already realized that the provisioning of Paris requires a freer circulation in the streets, and those who have erected the barricades have already in several places made openings large enough for the passage of wagons and carts. Let this example be imitated everywhere. Let Paris reassume its accustomed appearance and trade its activity and confidence. . . .

(b) Decree on the Position of Working Men

Source: Ibid., p. 58, in Robinson and Beard, pp. 80–81.

The provisional government of the French republic decrees that the Tuileries shall serve hereafter as a home for the veterans of labour.

The provisional government of the French republic pledges itself to guarantee the means of subsistence of the working man by labour.

It pledges itself to guarantee labour to all citizens.

It recognizes that working men ought to enter into associations among themselves in order to enjoy the advantage of their labour.

*   *   *

The provisional government of the French republic decrees that all articles pledged at the pawn shops since the first of February, consisting of linen, garments, clothes, etc., upon which the loan does not exceed ten francs, shall be given back to those who pledged them. The minister of finance is ordered to meet the payments incidental to the execution of the present edict.

The provisional government of the republic decrees the immediate establishment of national workshops. The minister of public works is charged with the execution of the present decree.

(c) The National Workshops

Louis Blanc here explains the failure of the scheme, interesting as an example of early Socialism.

Source: L. Blanc, *Historical Revelations* (1858), pp. 194 ff., in Robinson and Beard, pp. 82–84.

But what were these national workshops to be? A mere hazardous expedient, or a noble and vigorous experiment in the organization of labour; a temporary resource to meet the serious problem of the unemployed, or a starting point for social regeneration? M. Marie knew my opinions better than anyone else; for only a few days before the Revolution of February, in a rather numerous gathering of deputies and journalists in his own house, I had clearly explained them; and I may add, they had encountered no more decided opponent than M. Marie himself. And yet it was to him, who totally misunderstood and dreaded socialism, who had sworn in his heart to resist it, *à l'outrance*, that the organization of the national workshops was to be committed. The actual direction of the workshops, moreover, was intrusted to M. Émile Thomas, whom I did not even know by sight; and one of the claims which recommended that person was his ardent, indefatigable opposition to my doctrines. Later he officially testified, 'I have never spoken to M. Louis Blanc in my life; I don't know him.' Again, 'While I was at the head of the workshops I saw M. Marie daily, sometimes twice a day; never once M. Ledru Rollin, M. Louis Blanc, nor M. Albert.'

Nor let it be objected that, though these national workshops were not organized with my concurrence, they were, at all events, in conformity with my principles. The truth is precisely the reverse. In point of fact, it is monstrous to confound the industrial system developed in my *Organization of Labour* with the system of the national workshops managed by M. Émile Thomas, under the sanction of M. Marie.

The *social workshops*, such as I had suggested, were each of them to consist of workmen belonging to the same trade. The national workshops, as put in operation by M. Marie, consisted in a collection of workmen got together pellmell, and yet—absurd as it was!—all put to the same kind of work. In the social workshops, as suggested by me the workmen were to pursue their business, the State lending them capital, to be repaid according to certain stipulations; they, working exclusively for their own profit, with a view to a joint benefit, that is to say, with all the stimulus of personal interest, combined with the *esprit de corps* engendered by the pursuit of a common object.

In the *national workshops*, as managed by M. Marie, the State interfered simply as a contractor; the operatives worked only as paid instruments. Now, as the kind of labour in these workshops was utterly unproductive and absurd, besides being such as the greater part of the men were unaccustomed to, the State was simply squandering the public funds; its subsidies were a premium upon idleness; its wages, alms in disguise. The *social workshops*, as suggested by me, consisted of groups of workingmen, united by the most intimate ties and identity of interest; groups, therefore, seriously concerned in being industrious and in the highest degree productive. The *national workshops*, as managed by M. Marie, were nothing more than a rabble of paupers, whom it was enough to feed, since no one knew how to employ them, and who had to live together without any other ties than a military organization, and under chiefs who bore the name, at once so strange and yet so characteristic, of sergeant majors.

The national workshops emptied the exchequer at a dead loss; they humiliated the workingman, who was reduced to accept the bread which he desired to earn; they discredited State interference in industrial matters. In the place of associations of workmen they got together battalions of paid idlers,—a strange army, sooner or later to be disbanded at the risk of civil war! The believers in the doctrine of *laissez faire* had, of course, every reason for attempting to fix upon us the responsibility for all this mischief. What luck for the disciples of the old political economy, if they could succeed in playing a trick on public opinion; if they could contrive to pass off as the highest practical form of the organization of labour those 'national workshops', which were nothing more than its ignoble travesties!

4. The Second Empire, 1852–70

(a) 'The Empire Is Peace'

Napoleon was President of the 2nd Republic, following the coup d'état of December 1851, when he made this speech at Bordeaux on 9 October 1852.

Source: *Le Moniteur Universel*, 12 October 1852, in Robinson and Beard, pp. 91–92.

The purpose of this journey, as you know, was to see for myself our beautiful provinces of the south and familiarize myself with their needs. It has, however, given rise to a much more important result. Indeed,—and I say it with a candour as far removed from arrogance as from false modesty,—never has a people testified in a manner more direct, spontaneous and unanimous, the longing to be freed from anxiety as to the future by concentrating in a single person an authority which shall accord with their desires. They realize now both the false hopes with which they have been deluded and the dangers which threaten them. . . .

France today encompasses me with her sympathies because I do not belong to the group of dreamers. In order to benefit the country it is not necessary to resort to new systems, but, above all, to establish confidence in the present and security for the future. This is why France seems to wish to revert to the empire.

There is, nevertheless, one apprehension, and that I shall set at rest. A spirit of distrust leads certain persons to say that the empire means war. I say, the empire means peace. France longs for peace, and if France is satisfied, the world is tranquil. Glory is rightly handed down hereditarily, but not war. . . .

I concede, nevertheless, that, like the emperor, I have many conquests to make. I would, like him, conquer, for the sake of harmony, the warring parties and bring into the great popular current the wasteful and conflicting eddies. I would conquer, for the sake of religion, morality, and material ease, that portion of the population, still very numerous, which, in the midst of a country of faith and belief, hardly knows the precepts of Christ; which, in the midst of the most fertile country of the world, is hardly able to enjoy the primary necessities of life. We have immense uncultivated districts to bring under cultivation, roads to open, harbours to construct, rivers to render navigable, canals to finish, and our network of railroads to bring to completion. . . .

This is what I understand by the empire, if the empire is to be re-established. These are the conquests which I contemplate, and all of you who surround me, who like myself, wish the good of our common country, you are my soldiers.

(b) The Franco-Prussian War, 1870-71

Bismarck wrote this letter to his wife.

Source: Schilling, *Quellenbuch zur Geschichte der Neuzeit* (2nd ed.), p. 424, in Robinson and Beard, pp. 160-1.

Vendress, September 3, 1870.

Day before yesterday before daybreak I left my quarters here; today I am returning, and have in the meantime experienced the great battle of Sedan on the 1st; in which we made towards thirty thousand prisoners and forced back the rest of the French army (which we have been pursuing all the way from Bar-le-Duc) into the fortress, where they must surrender themselves along with the emperor. Yesterday morning at five o'clock, after I had been discussing until one o'clock in the morning with Moltke and the French generals the terms of the capitulation, General Reille, whom I know, awoke me to tell me that Napoleon wished to speak with me.

I rode, without washing and with no breakfast, towards Sedan, and found the emperor in an open carriage with three officers of high rank and three others on horseback on the highroad near Sedan. I dismounted, greeted him as politely as if we were in the Tuileries, and asked what were his Majesty's commands. He wished to see the king. I told him, as was the truth, that his Majesty had his quarters three miles from there, at the place where I am now writing. On Napoleon's asking whither he should go, I offered him, since I was unfamiliar with the region, my quarters at Donchéry, a little place in the neighbourhood close to Sedan. He accepted my invitation, and, accompanied by his six Frenchmen, myself and Karl,[1] who had in the meantime followed me, drove, in the silence of the morning, towards our forces.

Before we reached the place he began to be apprehensive lest he might encounter a number of people, and he asked me whether he could not get out at a lonely labourer's cottage on the road. I had the place inspected by Karl, who reported that it was miserable and dirty. 'N'importe,' said Napoleon; and I ascended with him a narrow, rickety stairway. In a room ten feet square, with a deal table and two rush-bottomed chairs, we sat an hour, while the others remained below,—a singular contrast to our last interview in '67 in the Tuileries.

Our negotiations were difficult, unless I consented to touch upon matters which could not but be painful to one who had been so cast down by God's mighty hand. I had

[1] Bismarck's son.

summoned officers, through Karl, from the town and had asked Moltke to come. We then sent out one of the former to reconnoitre, and discovered, half a mile away, in Fresnois, a little villa with grounds.

Thither I accompanied the emperor, with an escort from the king's cuirassier regiment, which had been called up in the meantime; and there we concluded, with the French general Wimpffen, the capitulation, according to which forty to sixty thousand French,—I cannot be more accurate at this time,—with all that they had, became our prisoners. Day before yesterday and yesterday cost France one hundred thousand men and an emperor. This morning the latter started with all the members of his court, his horses and carriages, for Wilhelmshöhe, near Cassel.

This has been an event of vast historic importance,—a victory for which we must thank the Lord in humbleness of heart. It decides the conflict, although we must still carry on the war against an emperorless France. . . .

Goodbye, my sweetheart. Love to the children.

Your v.B.

5. The Paris Commune of 1871

The government of Thiers made this appeal to Parisians to reject the Commune.

Source: Simon, *The Government of M. Thiers* (1879) I, 484 ff., in Robinson and Beard, p. 211.

The Government of the French Republic to the Parisians:

France, freely consulted by universal suffrage, has elected a government, which is the only legal one; the only one that can command obedience if universal suffrage is not an empty word. . . .

In spite of this government, the Commune—that is to say, the minority which oppresses you, and which dares to hoist the infamous red flag—presumes to impose its will upon France. By its works you will be able to judge of the régime to which it would destine you. It violates property, imprisons citizens to make hostages of them, turns your streets and your public places, once throbbing with the commerce of the world, into deserts; suspends labour in Paris, paralyses it throughout France; arrests the prosperity which was about to revive, retards the evacuation of territory by the Germans, and exposes you to fresh attacks on their part, which they are prepared to execute without mercy, unless we ourselves come and suppress the insurrection.

* * *

The government is well aware, from many sources, that as soon as the soldiers have entered the walls you will rally round the national flag and assist our army in the destruction of a sanguinary and cruel tyranny.

It depends upon yourselves to avert the disasters inseparable from an assault. You are a hundred times more numerous than the followers of the Commune. Join, then, and in a body open the gates to us, which they have closed against law, against order, against your own prosperity and that of France. The gates once open, the guns will be silenced at once; quiet, order, prosperity, and peace will return within your walls; the Germans will evacuate your territory, and the traces of your misfortunes will rapidly disappear.

But if you do not act, the government will be obliged to take the surest and promptest measures for your deliverance. It owes this to you, but it owes it above all to France, because the evils that weigh on you weigh on her, the paralysis of business that ruins you, extends to and equally ruins her. She has the right to be saved, even if you do not know how to save yourselves. Parisians, think seriously; in a very few days we shall be in Paris. France will make an

end of civil war. She will, she should, she can. She comes
to deliver you, you can contribute to your own safety by
rendering the assault needless, and by once more taking
your place amongst your brethren.

A more favourable picture of the aims emerges from this
speech to the Commune by its President, Charles Beslay, very
much a moderate, in April 1871.

Source: Translated in Jellinek, *The Paris Commune of 1871*
(1937), p. 176.

The enfranchisement of the Commune of Paris is the
enfranchisement, we cannot doubt, of all the communes in
the Republic . . . Your adversaries have said that you have
struck the Republic; we reply that if we have struck it, it
is as one strikes a pile, to drive it deeper into the ground . . .
The Republic today is not what it was in the great days of
our Revolution. The Republic of '93 was a soldier who, in
order to fight for its defence at home and abroad, needed
to centralise in its hands all the forces of the country; the
Republic of 1871 is a worker who above all needs liberty
in order to fertilise peace. *Peace and work!* There lies our
future! There lies the assurance of our vindication and our
social regeneration, and, understood in this sense, the
Republic may yet make of France the support of the weak,
the protector of the toiler, the hope of the oppressed of all
the world, the basis of the Universal Republic. . . . The
Commune will deal with local affairs; the Department
with regional; the Government with national. And let us
proclaim it aloud: the Commune that we are founding will
be the model Commune. There, in my opinion, citizens,
is the path to follow; enter upon it boldly and resolutely.
Let us not exceed the fixed limits of our programme, and
the country and the Government will be happy and proud
to applaud this revolution, so great, so simple, the most
fertile revolution in our history!

A grimmer picture of the issues is seen in this Proclamation of the Central Committee of the National Guard.

Source: Ibid., pp. 200–1.

Workers, do not be deceived: it is the great struggle: parasitism and labour, exploitation and production are at death-grips. If you are sick or vegetating in ignorance and squatting in the muck; if you want your children to be men gaining the reward of their labour, not a sort of animal trained for the workshop and for war, fertilising with their sweat the fortune of an exploiter or pouring out their blood for a despot; if you want the daughters whom you cannot bring up and watch over as you would to be no longer instruments of pleasure in the arms of the aristocracy of wealth; if you want debauch and poverty no longer to drive men to the police and women to prostitution; if, finally, you desire the reign of justice, workers, be intelligent, arise! and let your stout hands fling beneath your feet the foul reaction!

Citizens of Paris, merchants, industrialists, shopkeepers, thinkers, all of you that labour and seek in good faith the solution of social problems, the Central Committee adjures you to march united in progress. Take your inspiration from the destinies of our country and its universal genius.

The Central Committee firmly believes that the heroic people of Paris is about to immortalise itself and regenerate the world.

Long live the Republic! Long live the Commune!

6. The Third Republic, 1875–1918

(a) The Need for a Republic

By conviction Thiers was a royalist, but recognized the difficulties involved after the débâcle of 1871.

Source: F. Le Goff, *Life of Louis Adolphe Thiers* (1879), Appendix in Robinson and Beard, pp. 213–15.

In 1873, when the country saw the administrative system, the army, and the finances re-established, and the foreign enemy departed from our soil, a universal demand arose for the abandonment of the provisional form of government, and for the establishment of a permanent constitution, which meant, to give to each party, weary of waiting, the government of its choice. But there were three monarchical parties, and but one throne. The idea of gratifying them all had, therefore, to be abandoned. As for myself, my mind was made up. In the presence of these three competitors, monarchy was impossible. A republic was difficult without doubt, but possible if prudence and wisdom were exercised. Under a republic France had just been revived.

*   *   *

Now I ask every honest man, to whatever party he may belong, if the Count de Chambord could be placed on the throne, with the opinions that he professes and with the flag that he unfurls or if it is hoped that he may some day be acceptable after he has modified his views? We respect him too much to believe that he will do so. I will say nothing of the Orleans princes, who wish to be mentioned only after the Count de Chambord, according to their hereditary rank; but I ask if the country is ready to receive the Prince Imperial, who, though innocent of the misfortunes of France, suggests them so keenly that the nation still shudders at the bare mention of his name? . . .

Must France wait until her future masters are ready; until one candidate is brought over to other ways of thinking, until another has made an advance in his right of succession, and until a third has finished his education? In the meanwhile everything will be in suspense,—commerce, industry, finances, State affairs. How can business men be asked to engage in great industrial enterprises, and financiers to negotiate loans, when the future threatens fresh political troubles? And how can foreign cabinets be expected to strengthen their relations and form alliances with us, when French policy is liable to be directed by new chiefs and influenced by new ideas? . . .

We persistently ask if there be any other alternative than the following: either the monarchy, which is impossible, because there are three claimants and but one throne; or a republic, difficult to establish without doubt, not because of itself, but because of the opposition of the monarchical parties, but, nevertheless, possible, for it is supported by an immense majority of the people.

It is the duty, therefore, of this immense majority of the people to consult together, to unite and to vote against those who resist the establishment of the only government possible. Monarchy today, after the three revolutions that have overthrown it, would mean immediate civil war, if it were established now; and if put off for two years, or three years, the civil war is only postponed until that epoch. . . .

(b) The Motives behind French Imperialism

Many Frenchmen came to see in colonies a compensation for the loss of pre-eminence in Europe. One of the chief makers of this public opinion was Paul Leroy-Beaulieu (1843–1916), professor, economist, and writer.

Source: Works of Leroy-Beaulieu, quoted and translated in Agnes Murphy, *The Ideology of French Imperialism* (1948), pp. 140, 144; 168–9; 124, 126.

Grandeur

We were the first to explore the world; . . . we let ourselves be dispossessed not so much through weakness or powerlessness as through carelessness, negligence, contempt for slow-moving undertakings and postponed successes. Today, we possess Algeria; let us not be content to be established there: an occasion is offered to form there a laborious, respectable, devoted French population. Let us seize it: let us consecrate some of the funds from the national subscription to establish in Africa families from Alsace and Lorraine. . . .

. . . One of the great faults of our politics for almost the past two centuries has been that of looking upon France as a purely continental and European country, and of giving only a distracted attention to our distant possessions. If this false tendency had not prevailed for some generations, we would today hold a much more important place in the world than that which remains to us. . . .

* * *

. . . In the presence of a Germany which has fifty-five million inhabitants, which in twenty years will have sixty million, and in fifty, eighty million, and which can besides count on the support of the Austrians, all these hopes of revenge by force are true chimera, sentimental and patriotic, but singularly dangerous for the country. We must have on the continent only a purely defensive attitude; any idea of aggression, of interfering in the affairs of others ought to be banished from our imagination. . . .

* * *

. . . Let us open our eyes to the future; let us look into the middle of the twentieth century. Suppose that at that time we occupy Cochin China, Cambodia, Tonkin, and all of Annam; that in Africa, Algeria and Tunis, inhabited by more than three or four million Europeans and five or six million half-civilized Arabs, depend on our authority; that across the Sahara our influence has penetrated well into the Sudan, and that beyond we rejoin Senegal, do you not think that there would be in this a position more worthy of occupying us than the European complications from which we could never extract any gain? . . .

* * *

Economic

. . . It is, therefore, useful that in a country where capitalization is more rapid than elsewhere, a part of the annual savings should be transported to the new lands where they return more intense services and where they create a new demand for the manufacturing products of the mother country by offering to her as counterparts the raw products which are lacking to her. It is the most regular means of re-establishing an equilibrium which might have been destroyed; it is the sharpest spur to metropolitan production. . . .

. . . Thus we should congratulate ourselves on the expatriation of capital toward well-organized, prosperous colonies; this capital is not lost; it is rather multiplied; each one gains from its more productive employment on new soils; the colonies, the mother country, the entire world draw considerable advantages from it. It is, then, a short-sighted policy to blame the creation and upkeep of colonies because they cost either the government or individuals—in the last analysis, the nation—some millions in expenses for their establishment. . . .

*   *   *

. . . this is the second [economic advantage of colonization]: the opening up of new markets for the sale of the manufactured products of Europe, markets more profitable and of a greater extensibility than those to which we formerly had access, because new societies have a faculty of growth and facilities for the creation and the accumulation of riches infinitely greater than have the old societies. Thus, exchange becomes active and extended; the division of labour increases; industry having prospects of vaster markets can and must produce more, and this production on a larger scale evokes new improvements and new progress. . . .

. . . We are not taking a sufficient part in the invasion of the globe by the human race. We are insensibly effacing ourselves. There is still time to react against this stationary state, which would be a veritable decadence. The best means of re-animating fecundity in the French nation is to establish for ourselves outside markets. As long as we live withdrawn into ourselves, it is to be feared our number will not increase; let us then have wider horizons; let us assume a part in that exploitation of distant countries which attracts the English, the Germans, and the Russians. . . .

(c) The Dreyfus Case, 1894–1906

The document is the 'bordereau', undated and unsigned, on which Dreyfus was convicted in 1894. In November 1897 it was proved a forgery of Commandant Esterhazy, by Col. Picquart, new Chief of the Intelligence Section of the General Staff.

Source: Translated from G. Chapman, *The Dreyfus Case* (1955). Appendix.

Without news that you want to see me, I nevertheless send you, Sir, some interesting information.

1. A note on the hydraulic buffer of the 120 and the way in which this gun has behaved.

2. A note about the covering troops (a few modifications will be made by the new plan).

3. A note on a change in the artillery formations.

4. A note relating to Madagascar.

5. The draft Firing Manual of the Field Artillery (14th March 1894).

This last document is extremely hard to obtain, and I can only have it at my disposal for a very few days. The War Ministry has sent a fixed number to the Corps, and they are responsible for them. Each officer holding one must hand it back after manœuvres.

If, therefore, you will take from it what interests you, and keep it readily available for me afterwards, I will fetch it (je le prendrai)[2]. Unless you would like me to have it copied in extenso and send you what I have copied (la copie).

I am about to set off on manœuvres.

(d) The Entente Cordiale

The Entente Cordiale of 8 April 1904 was essentially a practical set of conventions settling specific differences over colonies, mainly in Egypt. This letter, below, from the British Foreign Secretary to the French Ambassador in 1912, shows how closely the British and French had come together, yet without specific commitment.

Source: Blue Book, *Great Britain and the European Crisis 1914*, pp. 56–57, in Mowat, *Select Treaties and Documents*, p. 15.

My dear Ambassador,

From time to time in recent years the French and British naval and military experts have consulted together. It has always been understood that such consultation does not restrict the freedom of either Government to decide at any future time whether or not to assist the other by armed force. We have agreed that consultation between experts is not, and ought not to be, regarded as an engagement that commits either Government to action in a contingency that has not arisen and may never arise. The disposition, for instance, of the French and British fleets respectively at the present moment is not based upon an engagement to co-operate in war.

You have, however, pointed out that if either Government had grave reason to expect an unprovoked attack by a third Power it might become essential to know whether

[2] [This is ambiguous, as it stands: either I will collect it (from you) or I will take it (from the office and let you have it).]

it could, in that event, depend upon the armed assistance of the other.

I agree that, if either Government had grave reason to expect an unprovoked attack by a third Power, or something that threatened the general peace, it should immediately discuss with the other whether both Governments should act together to prevent aggression and to preserve peace, and, if so, what measures they would be prepared to take in common. If these measures involved action, the plans of the general staffs would at once be taken into consideration, and the Governments would then decide what effect should be given to them.

Yours, etc.

E. Grey

7. The Third Republic, 1918-39

(a) Clemenceau's Attitude to Germany, 1919

J. M. Keynes (1883–1946), the great economist of the interwar years, was a severe critic of the Versailles peace.

Source: J. M. Keynes, *Essays in Biography*, pp. 6–7.

. . . His principles for the Peace can be expressed simply. In the first place, he was a foremost believer in the view of German psychology that the German understands and can understand nothing but intimidation, that he is without generosity or remorse in negotiation, that there is no advantage he will not take of you, and no extent to which he will not demean himself for profit, that he is without honour, pride, or mercy. Therefore you must never negotiate with a German or conciliate him: you must dictate to him. On no other terms will he respect you, or will you prevent him from cheating you. But it is doubtful how far he thought these characteristics peculiar to Germany, or whether his candid view of some other nations was fundamentally different. His philosophy had, therefore, no place for 'sentimentality' in international relations. Nations are real things, of which you love one and feel for the rest indifference—or hatred. The glory of the nation you love is a desirable end—but generally to be obtained at your neighbour's expense. The politics of power are inevitable, and there is nothing very new to learn about this war or the end it was fought for; England had destroyed, as in each preceding century, a trade rival; a mighty chapter had been closed in the secular struggle between the glories of Germany and of France. Prudence required some measure of lip service to the 'ideals' of foolish Americans and hypocritical Englishmen; but it would be stupid to believe that there is much room in the world, as it really is, for such affairs as the League of Nations, or any sense in the principle of self-determination except as an ingenious formula for rearranging the balance of power in one's own interests.

(b) The Occupation of the Ruhr, 1923

The Reparations Commission in Paris broke down on 4 January.

Source: *The Times*, Friday, 12 January 1923.

FRENCH IN ESSEN. STRONG FORCES EMPLOYED. SULLEN CROWDS.

From our Special Correspondent.
Essen, January 11th, 4.15 p.m.

Essen was occupied this afternoon by two divisions of French troops.

Many houses and shops had drawn their blinds, but until the railway station was reached, there was nothing unusual to be seen. Here large numbers of men were gathered in the square.

At twenty minutes to two, the main body of the French forces came down the hill to the railway station and chief post office. At the head rode a party of cyclists in dark blue uniform and steel helmets closely followed by five parti-coloured armoured cars. From these grim-looking cars, of which the occupants were invisible, stood out the muzzles of the machine guns, a silent threat to the sullen crowd.

Despite the machine guns, the swords, the slung rifles of the horizon blue cavalry, who came cantering down the street behind the armoured cars, there were angry murmurs from the crowd—many took no trouble to hide the hatred in their hearts. No one thought of his neighbour. Everyone's face was set in the effort to preserve his control or had already lost it in some cry of grief or pain.

The French troops behaved with absolute correctness—there was no hectoring and no jesting. As on a ceremonial, these men passed silently through the equally silent lanes of human beings. But the French rode as conquerors; some of the officers especially, could not but show their pride in military pomp. The silence was remarkable. Only the clattering of horses' hooves over the cobbles broke it.

At the Post Office, close to the station, a troop of cavalry halted, dismounted and unslung rifles. An officer sprang to the ground, drawn sword in hand and ran lightly up the steps followed by two troopers. In a trice the latter had crossed their rifles, barring alike ingress and exit. Two squads of infantry appeared as by magic and cleared the pavement. In vain did agitated Germans seek to argue with these men; they coldly thrust them back. Sword in hand still, the officer passed through the swing doors, formally to take over the administration.

The following extract from *The Times* of 11 January illustrates British and American reactions.

U.S. TROOPS RECALLED. ANGER AT FRENCH ACTION.

The President of the U.S.A. has decided that the time has come to complete the evacuation of the American army from Germany. . . . The official spokesman confined himself to a bare statement of the fact . . . and left the vehemence with which he spoke to indicate the official sense of the gravity of the moment.

(c) The Maginot Line

Source: *The New York Times*, 4 September 1938 (condensed).

The Maginot Line ran from Sedan near the Luxembourg border to Switzerland, along France's North-eastern frontier. When war came, the line was made useless by the very rapid advance of the German mechanised divisions, through Belgium and Holland. German divisions then surrounded the main French armies lying behind the Line.

The Maginot Line is pre-eminently a combination of passive obstacle and active defence; its building marked the abandonment of the 'offensive à outrance'—attack at all costs—which led to such tragic results in the Great War.

The fortifications hardly rise above the surface, and the line has been aptly termed 'the crust of the East'. Great precautions have been taken to assure the maximum of resistance for this crust. The towers of the underground workings are monolithic, and no shell can penetrate them. Defence against gas is assured by a special process; electric machinery maintains in the interior an atmospheric pressure slightly higher than the external pressure.

The gunners lay their guns without seeing anything, following the indications on a dial controlled by an artillery officer, who is in a hermetically sealed armoured chamber. They see the outside world through panoramic telescopes built into the armour plate.

* * *

Thus protected, the soldiers of the crust can resist the fiercest bombardments, and literally cover the frontier zone with a sheet of fire through which no infantry could possibly advance. The strength of the Maginot Line lies in the diversity of its works; the variety of dimensions and of camouflage is very great.

* * *

The line is permanently occupied by what French soldiers call 'écrevisses de rempart'. They wear a khaki beret whose badge is a shield with the device of the defenders of Verdun 'On ne passe pas!'

In peace time these men keep unceasing watch, and live the wartime life of the trenches, with its system of relief: fifteen days in the line, fifteen days of rest.

The men are unceasingly at work, stiffening the network of barbed wire and tending the so-called 'asparagus' beds. These latter are steel rails driven into the ground with their points upward, to arrest the progress of tanks. The rails are set at a slope, and at different heights, so that the tank see-saws as it scales them. And, while the rails are tearing off the caterpillar tracks, the anti-tank guns, at ground level, can fire directly into the interior of the tank.

* * *

French military circles express the utmost confidence that the Maginot Line is impregnable to all attack. But from it columns of German workmen may be seen busily erecting the Siegfried line which will certainly not be less strong.

The rôle of these two 'Chinese Walls' of the twentieth

century in any future war will, it goes without saying, be of the utmost importance.

(d) Reaction to the Threat from Germany, 1936

M. Sarraut, the French Prime Minister, denounced the re-occupation of the Rhineland in a broadcast of 8 March 1936.

Source: *Keesing's Contemporary Archives*, 1936, pp. 2019–20.

Germany freely contracted solemn engagements in 1925. She renewed the promises of the peace treaty concerning the demilitarisation of the Rhineland Zone. Obligations and promises are today repudiated.

. . . The Treaty of Locarno provides that if there is a difference between two countries on which they cannot agree, they will have the right to refer it to judges or to a conciliation committee. The German Government could have applied to The Hague Court. We had already declared publicly a fortnight ago that we were ready to submit to the arbitration of that body. . . . They did not do so. There again they broke their engagements. No one can believe that the circumstances called for any particular haste. Not even Germany . . .

It is true that in the document handed yesterday to the French Ambassador, the German Government, having violated their engagements, offered to contract new ones. I shall not consider these for two reasons. First, because the double example given us by the German government, within the space of a year, of the unilateral repudiation of solemn engagements can give us no confidence in their new proposals. The second reason is even more obvious. In contempt of the most established law, the German government sent important forces into the demilitarised zone . . . without having sought to enter into negotiations on the subject. We have been confronted with the *fait accompli* in its most brutal form.

Source: ibid., p. 2021.

The relevant Articles of the Versailles Treaty were:

Article 42. Germany is forbidden to maintain or construct any fortifications either on the left bank of the Rhine, or on the right bank to the west of a line drawn 50 kilometres to the East of the Rhine.

Article 43. In the area defined above, the maintenance and assembly of armed forces, either permanently or temporarily, and military manœuvres of any kind, as well as the upkeep of all permanent works of mobilization, are in the same way forbidden.

The relevant article of the Treaty of Locarno, October 1925. Source: ibid., p. 2021.

Article 1. The high contracting parties collectively and severally guarantee the maintenance of the territorial status quo . . . as fixed by or in pursuance of the Treaty of Peace signed at Versailles . . . and also the observance of the stipulations of articles 42 and 43 of the said treaty concerning the demilitarised zone.

(e) Changes of Ministry, 1938

The extract gives some idea of the rapid changes of ministry in France.

Source: *Keesing's Contemporary Archives, 1938*, p. 2900: compiled from *Le Temps, Le Matin, L'Œuvre, Le Populaire*.

M. Camille Chautemps handed his Cabinet's resignation to President Lebrun at 5.10 a.m. on January 14th, 1938.

The increasing industrial strife which has been evident in France during recent months, together with anxiety over the financial situation of the Republic, has led to the present grave political situation, which in some quarters is believed to herald the eventual break up of the 'Front Populaire'.

The events leading up to the downfall of the government . . . have been inaugurated by a statement made by M. Chautemps to the Chamber of Deputies on January 13th during which he severely condemned the labour unrest which has disturbed French industrial life in recent months. He declared that the Socialist and Communist sections of the 'Front' had not taken a strong enough line in opposing these disorders. At the same time he demanded support for a 'liberal financial policy' from the left wing groups involving no attempt at exchange control. Thereupon the Socialists and Communists met in joint consultation, after which M. Sérol, speaking for the Socialists, said they 'were unable to understand what the Prime Minister wanted of them'.

* * *

[14 January: M. Ramette, speaking for the Communists, in the Chamber] launched a demand for increased public expenditure, a sliding wage scale, increased unemployment pay and public works. . . .

[M. Chautemps replied] that at the very moment the government were insisting on financial prudence to save the franc, M. Ramette had found nothing better to do than bring up afresh the demand for vast expenditure.

M. Chautemps thereupon called for the suspension of the Chamber. . . . The Socialist Ministers decided almost immediately they must resign . . . the government as a whole followed suit.

* * *

After a day of incessant consultation, the President of the Republic asked M. Bonnet, Minister of Finance in the outgoing cabinet, to attempt the formation of a new cabinet. The latter tried in vain to form an administration. M. Lebrun had earlier, but without success, made the same request to M. Chautemps, M. Daladier (Minister of War) and M. Sarraut (Minister of State).

The Chautemps Cabinet had been in existence for six months and fourteen days, having succeeded the Blum Ministry on June 22nd, 1937.

[18 January 1938, the same M. Chautemps (Radical Socialist) formed a new administration, made up of Radical Socialists (with only two exceptions), and not, as before, of the Front Populaire parties.]

Germany

8. The German Confederation, 1815

These are some of the main provisions of the German Act of Confederation, 8 June 1815.

Source: Meyer, *Corpus juris confoederationis Germanicae* (2nd ed.), II, 3 ff., in Robinson and Beard, pp. 17–20.

Article I. The sovereign princes and free towns of Germany, including their Majesties the emperor of Austria and the kings of Prussia, of Denmark, and of the Netherlands; to wit, the emperor of Austria and the king of Prussia, for all of their possessions formerly belonging to the German Empire; the king of Denmark for Holstein; and the king of the Netherlands for the grand duchy of Luxemburg, unite in a perpetual union which shall be called the German Confederation.

II. The aim of the same shall be the maintenance of the external and internal safety of Germany and of the independence and inviolability of the individual German states.

III. All members of the union have, as such, equal rights. They all engage alike to maintain inviolate the Act of Confederation.

IV. The affairs of the Confederation shall be confided to a Diet of the Confederation, in which all members of the union shall vote through their plenipotentiaries, either individually or collectively, in the following manner, without prejudice to their rank.

[There follows a list of states—1 vote each.]

V. Austria shall preside in the Diet of the Confederation. Each member of the union has the right to make and support propositions, and the presiding state is bound within a determined period to bring them under deliberation.

*   *   *

XI. The members of the Confederation reserve to themselves the right of forming alliances of all kinds. They pledge themselves, however, to contract no engagement which shall be directed against the safety of the Confederation or that of any individual state within the union.

The members of the Confederation pledge themselves likewise not to make war among themselves upon any pretence, or to follow up their contentions with force, but to submit these to the Diet. It shall devolve upon this body to attempt arbitration by means of a commission. Should this fail and a judicial decision become necessary, the same shall be effected through a well-organized court of arbitration, to the decision of which the conflicting parties shall forthwith submit, without appeal.

9. The Revolution of 1848–49

Frederick William IV, King of Prussia, explains his rejection of the imperial crown (15 May 1849).

Source: Schilling, *Quellenbuch zur Geschichte der Neuzeit* (2nd ed.), p. 431, in Robinson and Beard, p. 111.

. . . In so serious and dangerous a crisis I am moved publicly to address a word to my people.

I was not able to return a favourable reply to the offer of a crown on the part of the German National Assembly, because the Assembly has not the right, without the consent of the German governments, to bestow the crown which they tendered me, and moreover, because they offered the crown upon condition that I would accept a constitution which could not be reconciled with the rights and safety of the German States.

I have exhausted every means to reach an understanding with the German National Assembly. . . . Now the Assembly has broken with Prussia. The majority of its members are no longer those men upon whom Germany looked with pride and confidence. The greater part of the deputies voluntarily left the Assembly when they saw that it was on the road to ruin, and yesterday I ordered all the Prussian deputies who had not already withdrawn to be recalled. The other governments will do the same.

A party now dominates the Assembly which is in league with the terrorists. While they urge the unity of Germany as a pretence, they are really fighting the battle of godlessness, perjury, and robbery, and kindling a war against monarchy; but if monarchy were overthrown, it would carry with it the blessings of law, liberty, and property. The horrors committed in Dresden, Breslau, and Elberfeld under the banner of German unity afford a melancholy proof of this. New horrors are occurring and are in prospect.

While such crimes have put an end to the hope that the Frankfort Assembly can bring about German unity, I have, with a fidelity and persistence suiting my royal station, never lost hope. My government has taken up with the more important German States the work on the German constitution begun by the Frankfort Assembly. . . .

This is my method. Only madness or deception will dare, in view of these facts, to assert that I have given up the cause of Germany unity, or that I am untrue to my earlier convictions and assurances. . . .

10. The Austro-Prussian War of 1866

Bismarck wrote his *Reflections and Reminiscences* after his retirement in 1890.

Source: Bismarck, *Gedanken und Erinnerungen*, in Robinson and Beard, pp. 148–50.

On July 23, under the presidency of the king, a council of war was held, in which the question to be decided was whether we should make peace under the conditions offered or continue the war. A painful illness from which I was suffering made it necessary that the council should be held in my room. On this occasion I was the only civilian in uniform. I declared it to be my conviction that peace must be concluded on the Austrian terms,—but remained alone in my opinion; the king supported the military majority.

My nerves could not stand the strain which had been put upon them day and night; I got up in silence, walked into my adjoining bedchamber, and was there overcome by a violent paroxysm of tears. Meanwhile I heard the council dispersing in the next room. I thereupon set to work to commit to paper the reasons which, in my opinion, spoke for the conclusion of peace, and begged the king, in the event of his not accepting the advice for which I was responsible, to relieve me of my functions if the war were continued.

* * *

We had to avoid wounding Austria too severely; we had to avoid leaving behind in her any unnecessary bitterness of feeling or desire for revenge; we ought rather to reserve the possibility of becoming friends again with our adversary of the moment, and in any case to regard the Austrian State as a piece on the European chessboard and the renewal of friendly relations as a move open to us. If Austria were severely injured, she would become the ally of France and of every other opponent of ours; she would even sacrifice her anti-Russian interests for the sake of revenge on Prussia.

On the other hand, I could not see any guarantee for us in the future of the countries constituting the Austrian monarchy, in case the latter were split up by risings of the Hungarians and Slavs or made permanently dependent on those peoples. What would be substituted for that portion of Europe which the Austrian state had hitherto occupied from Tyrol to Bukowina? Fresh formations on this territory could only be of a permanently revolutionary nature. German Austria we could neither wholly nor partly make use of. The acquisition of provinces like Austrian Silesia and portions of Bohemia could not strengthen the Prussian State; it would not lead to an amalgamation of German Austria with Prussia, and Vienna could not be governed from Berlin as a mere dependency.

. . . To all this the king raised no objection, but declared the actual terms as inadequate, without, however, definitely formulating his own demands. Only so much was clear, that his claims had grown considerably since July 4. He said that the chief culprit could not be allowed to escape unpunished, and that, justice once satisfied, we could let the misled backsliders off more easily; and he insisted on the cessions of territory from Austria which I have already mentioned.

I replied that we were not there to sit in judgment, but to pursue the German policy. Austria's conflict and rivalry with us were no more culpable than ours with her; our task was the establishment or foundation of German national unity under the leadership of the king of Prussia.

Passing on to the German States, the king spoke of various acquisitions by cutting down the territories of all our opponents. I repeated that we were not there to administer retributive justice, but to pursue a policy; that I wished to avoid in the German federation of the future the sight of mutilated territories, whose princes and peoples might very easily (such is human weakness) retain a lively wish to recover their former possessions by means of foreign aid.

11. The Franco-Prussian War, 1870-71

(a) The Ems Telegram

Modern historians suggest that Bismarck improved on the facts in this account taken from his *Gedanken*, to stress his own ability and foresight.

Source: Bismarck, *Gedanken und Erinnerungen*, II, 256.

. . . All these considerations, whether conscious or unconscious, strengthened my impression that the war could not be avoided except at the cost of both our Prussian honour and the national faith in it.

With this conviction I made use of the royal authorization, which Abeken[3] had transmitted to me, to publish the contents of the telegram, and in the presence of both my guests I reduced the telegram, by omissions, to the following version without, however, adding or altering even one word.

'After the news of the resignation of the Hereditary Prince of Hohenzollern had been officially communicated by the Royal Spanish to the Imperial French Government, the French ambassador in Ems had requested His Majesty the King to authorize him that he may wire to Paris that His Majesty the King had pledged himself for all future times nevermore to give his consent if the Hohenzollern should revert to their candidature. At that His Majesty the

[3] A Foreign Office representative who often accompanied the king.

King has refused to receive the French ambassador again and has told him through the adjutant on duty that His Majesty has nothing further to convey to the ambassador.'

The difference in the effect of the shortened version of the Ems Telegram as compared to the one the original would have produced, was not the result of stronger words but of the form, which made this announcement appear conclusive, while Abeken's wording would merely have seemed the fragment of a negotiation pending and to be continued in Berlin.

When I had read out the contracted version to my two guests, Moltke remarked: 'Now that has another sound; before it sounded like a signal for retreat, now like a fanfare in response to a challenge.' I explained: 'If, in execution of His Majesty's order, I at once communicate this text, which contains no alterations and no addition to the telegram, not only to the newspapers but also to all our embassies, it will be known in Paris before midnight and not only because of its contents, but also by the way of its publication, its effect there will be that of a red cloth on the Gallic bull. Fight we must unless we wish to play the part of the vanquished without a fight. Success, however, depends essentially on the impression which the origin of the war will produce in ourselves and in others; it is important that we are the attacked—and Gallic pride and irascibility will make us that—once we proclaim in front of the European public, so far as we can do it without the mouthpiece of the Reichstag, that we fearlessly stand up to the open threats of France.'

This exposition of mine caused a turn of cheerfulness in both generals which surprised me by its vivacity. Suddenly they had regained their appetite for food and drink and were talking in a merry vein. Roon said: 'The old God is still alive and will not let us go down in ignominy.' Moltke went so far out of his detached passivity that with a glad look towards the ceiling, and abandoning his usual reserve in words, he beat his chest with his hand and said: 'If I am to live to see that, to lead our armies in such a fight, then afterwards the devil may take the old carcass at once.' He was at the time more frail than later and doubtful whether he would survive the hardships of the campaign.

(b) Proclamation of the German Empire, 18 January 1871

Source: *Der Krieg Deutschlands gegen Frankreich* (1871), pp. 812 ff., in Robinson and Beard, pp. 163–5.

In the palace of Louis XIV, in that ancient centre of a hostile power which for centuries has striven to divide and humiliate Germany, the solemn proclamation of the German Empire was made on January 18th, exactly one hundred and seventy years after the assumption of the royal dignity by the Prussian sovereigns at Konigsberg. Though the German people, owing to the necessities of the times, were represented at the ceremony only by the German army, the eyes of the entire nation were gratefully turned to the place where, surrounded by sovereigns, generals, and soldiers, King William announced to the world the assumption by himself and his heirs of a title for the re-establishment of which we have been yearning during the sixty long years it has been in abeyance.

As yet the infatuation of the enemy does not permit us to throw aside the weapons we have taken up in self-defence; and as our unity arose out of the first part of the campaign, so will our empire be strengthened by the remaining feats of arms. By the self-sacrificing devotion of all classes of society, the nation has proved that it still possesses that warlike prowess which distinguished our ancestors. It has recovered its ancient position in Europe;

and, neither fearing an adversary nor envying any neighbour, discreet and temperate in its acts and aims, it accepts the destiny prophesied for it in the proclamation of its new emperor. This destiny is to add to its power not by conquest but by promoting culture, liberty, and civilization. As far as the German people are concerned, there will be no more wars in Europe after the termination of the present campaign. . . .

Owing to the unfavourable weather, the festive procession which was to conduct His Majesty from the prefecture to the palace did not take place. The crown prince, with Lieutenant General Blumenthal, his chief of staff, and an escort of Prussians, Wurtembergers, Badeners, and Bavarians, drove to the palace to receive his royal father at the eastern portal in front of the Princes' Stairway. In the courtyard of the palace a company of the king's own troops was drawn up as a guard of honour. . . .

At a quarter past twelve His Majesty entered the hall, when a choir consisting of men of the Seventh, Forty-Seventh, and Fifty-Eighth regiments intoned the choral, 'Let all the world rejoice in the Lord.' . . . When the choir ceased, the congregation sang one verse of the choral, 'Praise and honour unto the Lord.' The ordinary military liturgy was then read by the clergymen and a sermon preached by the Reverend A. Rogge. Alluding to the well-known inscription on the ceiling of the hall, 'Le roi governe par lui-même', the preacher observed that the kings of Prussia had risen to greatness by adopting a different and more religious motto, namely, 'The kings of the earth reign under me, saith the Lord.' The Te Deum Laudamus closed the service.

The king then walked up to where the colours were displayed, and, standing before them, read the document proclaiming the re-establishment of the German Empire. Count Bismarck having read the King's proclamation to the German nation, the grand duke of Baden stepped forth and exclaimed, 'Long live His Majesty the emperor!' The cheers of the assembly were taken up by the bands playing the national anthem.

12. Bismarck, 1870–90

Extracts from (a) the Anti-socialist Law of 1878 and (b) a Government Report of 1904 on the Workings of Bismarck's Social Legislation

Sources: Russell, *German Social-Democracy*, pp. 100 ff.; German Government's official *Report at St. Louis Exhibition*, pp. 339 ff., in Robinson and Beard, pp. 187–92.

Associations which aim, by social-democratic, socialistic, or communistic agitation, at the destruction of the existing order in State or society are forbidden. . . .

Meetings in which social-democratic, socialistic, or communistic tendencies, directed to the destruction of the existing order in State or society, make their appearance are to be dissolved. Such meetings as appear to justify the assumption that they are destined to further such tendencies are to be forbidden. Public festivities and processions are placed under the same restrictions.

All printed matter, in which appear social-democratic, socialistic, or communistic tendencies, directed to the destruction of the existing order in State and society in a manner dangerous to the peace and, in particular, to the harmony between different classes of the population, is to be forbidden. In the case of periodical literature, the prohibition can be extended to any further issue, as soon as a single number has been forbidden under this law.

The collection of contributions for the furthering of social-democratic, socialistic, or communistic endeavours, directed toward the destruction of the existing order in

State or society, as also the public instigation to the furnishing of such contributions, are to be forbidden by the police. . . . The money seized from forbidden collections, or the equivalent of the same, is to fall to the poor-relief fund of the neighbourhood.

For districts or localities which are, owing to the above-mentioned agitation, threatened with danger to the public safety, the following provisions can be made, for the space of a year at most, by the central police of the State in question, and subject to the permission of the Bundesrath.

(1) That public meetings may only take place with the previous permission of the police; this prohibition does not extend to meetings for an election to the Reichstag or the diet.

(2) That the distribution of printed matter may not take place in public roads, streets, squares, or other public localities.

(3) That residence in such districts or localities can be forbidden to all persons from whom danger to the public safety or order is to be feared.

(b) The minimum of relief in case of sickness entitles the beneficiary to free medical treatment and medicine for 26 weeks; and in case of incapacity for work, financial assistance to the extent of one half of the average daily wage, or to free hospital nursing, besides one half of the allowance for those dependent on the sick person. Further, it entitles sick women to relief for six months after their confinement; and in case of death, burial money amounting to twenty times their average daily wage.

The necessary means are raised by weekly contributions (not higher than four per cent of the average wage), two thirds of which is borne by the insured and one third by the employer. The administration is carried out through sickness clubs organized according to trades or localities, whose presiding officers are chosen from the insured and the employers according to the ratio of the contributions. The insurance against sickness embraces (inclusive of the miners' clubs) about ten million persons in more than twenty thousand clubs, and involves an annual expenditure of about 200 million marks.

Insurance against accidents replaces the old law of Employers' Liability (its many defects being equally harmful to employer and employed) by a legal provision, which also insures the person injured, or his survivors, in cases of casual accidents, or such as have occurred through the fault of his co-workers, or through his own carelessness. . . .

* * *

Insurance against disablement and old age, which was introduced on the first of January, 1891, by an imperial law (revised in 1899), completes the system of workmen's insurance. . . . The insurance entitles those incapable of work to pensions without regard to age, and gives old-age pensions to septuagenarians regardless of working ability. . . .

The funds necessary for this insurance are raised through a yearly contribution from the government of fifty marks for each pension, together with weekly contributions to an equal amount from employer and employed. . . .

* * *

Instead of smothering the free initiative of self-helping bodies, as many had feared workmen's insurance would do, it has, on the contrary, enabled them to develop to their highest powers.

The reserve capital of 1,500,000,000 marks has furnished the means for solving the most important social economical questions.

Up to the end of 1902 over 400,000,000 marks had been expended from the funds of disablement-insurance institutions for the construction of workmen's dwellings, sick and convalescent houses, sanatoriums, public hospitals, homes for travelling workmen, public baths, blind asylums, kindergartens, slaughterhouses, systems of water works, sewerage and draining plants, street paving, savings banks, cooperative stores, and similar institutions for public welfare, as well as for the payment of agricultural loans (mortgages, light railroads, land and road improvement, development of cattle breeding, etc.), all measures the final aim of which is to cause the masses of the people to participate to an ever-increasing degree in the advance of civilization.

The advantages of German workmen's insurance, in distinction to other systems, is that:

(1) It guarantees the support required by necessitous persons immediately, and as a well-earned right.

(2) It gives both employer and employee common interests in their duties, and thereby acts in a way as an instrument of social reconciliation.

(3) It awakes a feeling of social duty throughout the nation, and

(4) It strengthens the working and defensive power of the nation.

(c) Foreign Policy after 1871: General Considerations

Source: Bismarck, *Gedanken und Erinnerungen*, II, 294–6.

If Germany has the advantage that her policy is free of direct interests in the East, on the other hand there is the disadvantage of the central and exposed position of the German Empire, with its extended frontier which has to be defended on all sides, and the ease with which anti-German coalitions are made. At the same time, Germany is perhaps the single Great Power in Europe which is not tempted by any objects obtainable only by a successful war. It is our interest to maintain peace. . . .

. . . That respect for the rights of other states in which France especially has always been lacking at the time of her supremacy, and which in England lasts only so long as English interests are not touched, is made easy for the German Empire . . . in that we do not require an increase in our immediate territory. It has always been my ideal aim, after we had established our unity to win the confidence not only of the smaller European states but also of the Great Powers, and to convince them that German policy would be just and peaceful, now that we had repaired the divisions of the nation. . . . During the time I was in office, I advised three wars . . . but each time I first made it clear to myself whether the war, if successful, would bring a prize of victory worthy the sacrifices which are now so much greater than in the last century.

(d) Foreign Policy after 1871: The Origins of the Dual Alliance, 1879

This extract is taken from a letter written by Bismarck to King Ludwig of Bavaria, dated Gastein, 10 September 1879.

Source: Bismarck, op. cit., pp. 268–70.

. . . Under these circumstances [Russian ambitions in the Balkans], I cannot resist the conviction that in the future, perhaps even in the near future, the peace is threatened by Russia and by Russia alone. It is true that according to our reports enquiries whether Russia, if she started a war, would find assistance in France and Italy, have produced a negative result. Italy has been found powerless and France has declared that she does not want a war now and that in alliance with Russia alone she would not feel herself strong enough for an offensive war against Germany.

In this situation Russia has during the last weeks made demands to us to the effect that we should definitely make our option between Russia and Austria. . . .

. . . Austria feels just as ill at ease in view of the restlessness of Russian politics as we do, and she seems inclined to come to an understanding with us for the purpose of jointly resisting any Russian attack against either of the two powers.

I should consider it as an essential guarantee of the peace of Europe and of Germany's safety, if the German Empire entered into such an agreement with Austria which would have for its object, now as before, carefully to cultivate the peace with Russia, yet to assist each other if, nevertheless, either of the two powers were to be attacked. In possession of such a mutual assurance both empires could, now as before, devote themselves to the renewed consolidation of the Three Emperors' Alliance. The German Empire in alliance with Austria would not lack the support of England, and in view of the pacific policy of these two big political bodies it could guarantee the peace of Europe with two million combatants. Neither could the purely defensive character of that mutual support between the two German powers be provocative to anybody, because the same mutual reassurance has already been in existence for fifty years, according to international law, through the relationship of the German Confederation of 1815.

If any agreement of that sort fails to be reached, nobody will be in a position to blame Austria if, under the pressure of Russian threats and without certainty as regards Germany, she tries to come into closer contact with either France or Russia. In the latter case Germany would be exposed, in view of her relations with France, to complete isolation on the Continent. If, however, Austria were to get in touch with France and England, as in 1854, Germany would become dependent on Russia alone and, if she did not want to isolate herself, tied to the courses, unsound and dangerous as I fear, of Russia's internal and external politics.

If Russia forces us to choose between herself and Austria, then I believe that Austria would indicate to us the conservative and peaceloving direction, Russia, however, an uncertain one.

* * *

13. The Post-Bismarck Empire, 1890-1918

(a) The German Navy

Prince von Bulow was Chancellor 1900-9.

Source: von Bulow, *Imperial Germany*, tr. M. A. Lewenz (1914), pp. 16-21.

The sea has become a factor of more importance in our national life than ever before in our history, even in the great days of the German Hansa. It has become a vital nerve which we must not allow to be severed if we do not wish to be transformed from a rising and youthfully vigorous people into a decaying and ageing one. But we were exposed to this danger as long as our foreign commerce and our mercantile marine lacked national protection at sea against the superior navies of other powers.

When in 1864 the English ambassador . . . let fall the remark that if Prussia did not cease operations against Denmark the English government might be forced to take arms against her, Herr von Bismarck-Schönhausen replied 'Well, what harm can you do us? At worst you can throw a few bombs at Stolpmünde or Pillau, and that is all.' Bismarck was right at that time . . . we possessed neither a great mercantile marine, the destruction of which could

sensibly injure us, nor any overseas trade worth mention-
ing, the crippling of which we need fear.

Today, it is different. We are now vulnerable at sea. We
have entrusted millions to the ocean, and with these
millions the weal and woe of many of our countrymen. . . .

The Building of the Fleet

Ever since the end of the eighties in the nineteenth
century the building of a fleet sufficient to defend our
overseas interests had been a vital question for the German
nation. It is greatly to the credit of the Emperor William II
that he recognized this and devoted all the power of the
throne and all the strength of his own personality to the
attainment of this end. . . .

. . . Parliamentary opposition, which was at that time
considerable, could only be overcome if steady pressure
were brought to bear on Parliament by public opinion.

. . . it was only possible to rouse public opinion by
harping on nationalism and waking the people to consciousness. A great oppression which weighed on the
spirit of the nation had been occasioned by the rupture[4]
. . . and could only be lifted if the German Emperor
could set before his people . . . a new goal towards which
to strive, and could indicate to them 'a place in the sun' to
which they had a right and which they must try to attain.
On the other hand, patriotic feeling must not be roused to
such an extent as to damage irreparably our relations with
England against whom our sea power would be for many
years insufficient. . . . To make it possible to build a
sufficient fleet was the foremost and greatest task of German policy after Bismarck's retirement; a task with which
I was immediately confronted when, on June 28th, 1897,
at Kiel, on board the 'Hohenzollern' I was entrusted by

[4] Of Bismarck and the Emperor.

His Majesty the Emperor, with the conduct of foreign affairs. . . .

. . . On November 27th, 1897, after Admiral Hollman, till then Secretary of State at the Imperial Admiralty Office, had been replaced by a man of first rate capabilities, Admiral von Tirpitz, the Government brought out a new Navy Bill which demanded the construction of seven additional ships of the line, of two large and seven small cruisers, and fixed the date of completion for the end of 1904.

(b) The Agadir Crisis, 1911

Lloyd George, Chancellor of the Exchequer in Asquith's Liberal Ministry, made the attitude of the British Government clear in a speech at the Mansion House.

Source: Quoted in A. W. Ward and C. P. Gooch, *The Cambridge History of British Foreign Policy 1783–1919*, pp. 445–6.

[The Foreign Secretary, Sir Edward Grey, explained how the Mansion House speech came to be made:]

In the course of that day, July 21st, the Chancellor of the Exchequer told me that he had to make a speech on an occasion of importance at the Mansion House the same evening. He consulted the Prime Minister and me as to what should be said. It was fourteen days since the last public statement from Morocco had been made here. . . . We were anxious as to the way things were developing, and we all three felt that for a Cabinet Minister of first rate importance to make a speech on a formal occasion and to say no word about Foreign Affairs after the interview[5] would be misleading to public opinion here and everywhere.

[Mr. Lloyd George said in his speech:]

[5] With the German Ambassador.

I am bound to say this, that I believe it is essential in the higher interests not merely of this country but of the world, that Britain should at all hazards maintain her place and her prestige amongst the Great Powers of the world. If a situation were to be forced on us in which peace could only be preserved by the surrender of the great and beneficent position Britain has won by centuries of heroism and achievements, by allowing Britain to be treated, where her interests were vitally affected, as if she were of no account in the Cabinet of Nations, then I say emphatically that peace at that price would be a humiliation intolerable for a great country like ours to endure.

(c) The Invasion of Belgium

Von Moltke the Younger, Chief of the General Staff in succession to Graf Schlieffen (1891–1905), wrote this commentary on the Schlieffen Plan probably in 1911, accepting its main premises.

Source: G. Ritter, *The Schlieffen Plan* (1958), pp. 165–6.

Comments on the memorandum by General von Moltke:

It may be safely assumed that the next war will be a war on two fronts. Of our enemies, France is the most dangerous and can prepare the most quickly. Accounts must be settled with her very soon after deployment. Should the defeat of the French be achieved quickly and decisively, it will also be possible to make forces available against Russia. I agree with the basic idea of opening the war with a strong offensive against France while initially remaining on the defensive with weak forces against Russia. If a quick decision is sought against France, the attack should not be directed exclusively against the strongly fortified eastern front of that country. If, as may be expected, the French army remains on the defensive behind that front, there is no chance of quickly breaking through; and even a break-through would expose the German army, or those sections which have made it, to flank attack from two sides. If one wants to meet the enemy in the open, the fortified frontier-line must be out-flanked. This is only possible by means of an advance through Switzerland or Belgium. The first would en-counter great difficulties and, because of the defence of the mountain roads, would take a long time. On the other hand a successful outflanking of the French fortifications would have the advantage of forcing the French army to-wards the north. An advance through Belgium would force the French back into their interior. Nevertheless it should be preferred, because there one can count on quicker progress. We can count on the somewhat in-efficient Belgian forces being quickly scattered, unless the Belgian army should withdraw without a battle to Ant-werp, which would then have to be sealed off.

It is important, of course, that for an advance through Belgium the right wing should be made as strong as possible. But I cannot agree that the envelopment de-mands the violation of Dutch neutrality in addition to Belgian. A hostile Holland at our back could have dis-astrous consequences for the advance of the German army to the west, particularly if England should use the violation of Belgian neutrality as a pretext for entering the war against us. A neutral Holland secures our rear, because if England declares war on us for violating Belgian neu-trality she cannot herself violate Dutch neutrality. She cannot break the very law for whose sake she goes to war.

14. The Weimar Republic, 1919-33

Gustav Stresemann was Chancellor for 100 stormy days in 1923, and then Foreign Minister in successive Cabinets until his death in 1929. The extract is from a speech made in

London at the signing of the Locarno treaties, 1 December 1925.

Source: *G. Stresemann: His Diaries, Letters and Papers*, II, p. 239, tr. Eric Sutton.

I should like to express to you, Herr Briand, my deep gratitude for what you said about the necessity of the co-operation of all peoples—and especially of those peoples that have endured so much in the past. You started from the idea that every one of us belongs in the first instance to his own country, and should be a good Frenchman, German, Englishman, as being a part of his own people, but that everyone also is a citizen of Europe, pledged to the great cultural idea that finds expression in the concept of our continent. We have a right to speak of a European idea; this Europe of ours has made such vast sacrifices in the Great War, and yet it is faced with the danger of losing, through the effects of that Great War, the position to which it is entitled by tradition and development.

The sacrifices made by our continent in the World War are often measured solely by the material losses and destruction that resulted from the War. Our greatest loss is that a generation has perished from which we cannot tell how much intellect, genius, force of act and will, might have come to maturity, if it had been given to them to live out their lives. But together with the convulsions of the World War one facet has emerged, namely that we are bound to one another by a single and a common fate. If we go down, we go down together; if we are to reach the heights, we do so not by conflict but by common effort.

For this reason, if we believe at all in the future of our peoples, we ought not to live in disunion and enmity, we must join hands in common labour. Only thus will it be possible to lay the foundations for a future of which you, Herr Briand, spoke in words that I can only emphasize, that it must be based on a rivalry of spiritual achievement, not of force. In such co-operation the basis of the future must be sought. The great majority of the German people stands firm for such a peace as this. Relying on this will to peace, we set our signature to this treaty. It is to introduce a new era of co-operation among the nations. It is to close the seven years that followed the War, by a time of real peace, upheld by the will of responsible and far-seeing statesmen, who have shown us the way to such development, and will be supported by their peoples, who know that only in this fashion can prosperity increase. May later generations have cause to bless this day as the beginning of a new era.

15. Hitler, 1933-39

(a) On Race

Mein Kampf was written in the Fortress of Landsberg am Lech in 1924 during Hitler's imprisonment there.

Source: *Mein Kampf*, tr. James Murphy, pp. 274-5.

If we review all the causes which contributed to bring about the downfall of the German people we shall find that the most profound and decisive cause must be attributed to the lack of insight into the racial problem and especially in the failure to recognize the Jewish danger.

It would have been easy enough to endure the defeats suffered on the battlefields in August 1918. They were nothing when compared with the military victories which our nation had achieved. Our downfall was not the result of those defeats; but we were overthrown by that force which had prepared those defeats by systematically operating for several decades to destroy those political instincts and that moral stamina which alone enable a people to struggle for its existence and therewith secure the right to exist.

By neglecting the problem of preserving the racial foundations of our national life, the old Empire abrogated the sole right which entitles a people to live on this planet. Nations that make mongrels of their people or allow their people to be turned into mongrels sin against the Will of Eternal Providence. And thus their overthrow at the hands of a stronger opponent cannot be looked upon as a wrong but, on the contrary, as a restoration of justice. If a people refuses to guard and uphold the qualities with which it has been endowed by Nature and which have their roots in the racial blood, then such a people has no right to complain over the loss of its earthly existence.

* * *

But the loss of racial purity will wreck inner happiness for ever. It degrades men for all time to come. And the physical and moral consequences can never be wiped out.

(b) On the Historic Rôle of Germany

Speech at Nuremberg, September 1933.

Source: *Hitler's Speeches, 1922–1929*, tr. N. H. Baynes, I, pp. 480–1.

Insofar then as we devote ourselves to the care of our own blood—that blood which has been entrusted to us by destiny—we are at the same time doing our best to help to safeguard other peoples from diseases which spring from race to race, from people to people. If in West or Central Europe but one single people were to fall a victim to Bolshevism, this poison would continue its ravages, it would devastate the oldest, the fairest civilization which can today be found upon this earth.

Germany by taking upon itself this conflict does but

fulfil, as so often before in her history, a truly European mission.

(c) On the Jews

Speech of 1922.

Source: Baynes, I, p. 30.

. . . The Jews are a people of robbers. He has never founded any civilization, though he has destroyed civilizations by the hundred. He possesses nothing of his own creation to which he can point. Everything that he has is stolen. Foreign peoples, foreign workmen build him his temples, it is foreigners who create and work for him: it is foreigners who shed their blood for him. He knows no 'people's army': he has only hired mercenaries who are ready to go to death on his behalf. He has no art of his own: bit by bit he has stolen it all from the other peoples or has watched them at work and then made his copy. He does not even know how merely to preserve the precious things which others have created: as he turns the treasures over in his hand they are transformed into dirt and dung. He knows that he cannot maintain any State for long. That is one of the differences between him and the Aryan. . . .

(d) On the Nazi Party

This speech was made to the Industry Club in Düsseldorf, 27 January 1932, and by it Hitler won the support of West German industrialists.

Source: Baynes, I, pp. 822–3.

* * *

. . . And today that Movement cannot be destroyed: it is there: people must reckon with it, whether they like it or not. (Loud applause) . . . For here they see before them an organization . . . inspired to the highest degree by national sentiment, constructed on the conception of an absolute authority in the leadership in all spheres, at every stage—the solitary party which amongst its members has completely overcome not only the conception of internationalism but also the idea of democracy, which in its entire organization acknowledges only the principles of Responsibility, Command, and Obedience. . . . Here is an organization which is filled with an indomitable aggressive spirit, an organization which when a political opponent says 'your behaviour we regard as a provocation' for the first time does not see fit immediately to retire from the scene but brutally enforces its own will and hurls against the opponent the retort, 'We fight today! We fight tomorrow! And if you regard our meeting today as a provocation we shall hold yet another next week—until you have learned that it is no provocation when *German* Germany also professes its belief!' And when you say "You must not come into the street" we go into the street in spite of you. And when you say 'Then we shall kill[6] you', however many sacrifices you force upon us, this young Germany will always continue its marches, and one day it will completely reconquer for the Germans the German street. And when people cast in our teeth our intolerance, we proudly acknowledge it—yes, we have formed the inexorable decision to destroy Marxism in Germany down to its very last root.

(e) The Occupation of the Rhineland, 7 March 1936

Source: *The Times*, Monday, 9 March 1936 (condensed).

WATCH ON THE RHINE.
STRENGTH OF NEW GARRISONS.
CROWD'S GREETINGS.

Frankfurt, March 8th.

[6] German: *schlagen.*

The main impression gained in the course of a rapid journey down the Rhine as far as Cologne yesterday, was that the Rhinelanders were astonished by the suddenness of the military occupation.

The troops had begun to move during the early hours of Saturday. The first units had quietly reached the precincts of the Rhenish towns before midday and partly crossed the Rhine bridges while Herr Hitler was still addressing the Reichstag. The other garrisons were occupied later in the afternoon and in the course of today. It was the sudden appearance of air squadrons over Cologne and Dusseldorf before noon on Saturday that gave the first sign to the Rhineland population that an historic hour had come.

The scenes which followed were everywhere the same. No sooner had the news spread and been confirmed over the radio than every house and building in the garrison towns was covered with flags within a few minutes. At Cologne the population rushed out of their homes, offices and factories to greet the first German troops to enter the city for eighteen years. At 10 o'clock the troops crossed the Hohenzollern Bridge, and presented a picture of excellent physical fitness and military smartness. With smiling faces and decorated with flowers they constantly exchanged greetings with the population, and finally aroused the crowds in the Dornplatz to a frantic enthusiasm when they marched past General von Kluge, the Commander of the VI Army Corps, who took the salute.

Source: *The Times*, 9 March.

Hitler was saying this as the troops moved in:

In this historic hour, when German troops are taking possession of their future peacetime garrisons in Germany's western provinces, we unite to testify to two holy innermost articles of faith.

57

First, to the oath to yield to no power or force in the re-establishment of the honour of our nation.

Secondly to the affirmation that we shall now all the more work for European understanding and particularly for an understanding with the Western powers and our Western neighbours.

After three years I believe that I can regard the struggle for German equality as concluded today. I believe, moreover, that thereby the first and foremost reason for our withdrawal from European collective security has ceased to exist—we have no territorial demands to make in Europe. We know that all the tensions which arise from wrong territorial provisions or the disproportion between the sizes of national population and their living room cannot be solved in Europe by war.

We hope that human wisdom will help to alleviate the pains of this condition, and allay the tensions by the method of gradual evolution in friendly cooperation.

(f) The Munich Settlement, 1938

At the conclusion of the Munich meeting, Hitler and Neville Chamberlain met alone except for an interpreter, and signed the following document, on 30 September 1938.

Source: W. S. Churchill, *The Second World War* (1948), I, p. 285.

We, the German Fuehrer and Chancellor, and the British Prime Minister, have had a further meeting today, and are agreed in recognising that the question of Anglo-German relations is of the first importance for the two countries and for Europe.

We regard the Agreement signed last night, and the Anglo-German Naval Agreement, as symbolic of the desire of our two peoples never to go to war with one another again.

We are resolved that the method of consultation shall be

the method adopted to deal with any other questions that may concern our two countries, and we are determined to continue our efforts to remove possible sources of difference, and thus to contribute to assure the peace of Europe.

Winston Churchill summed up the views of the anti-Munich minority in a speech to the House of Commons.

Source: op. cit., pp. 293–4.

We really must not waste time after all this long debate upon the difference between the positions reached at Berchtesgaden, at Godesberg, and at Munich. They can be very simply epitomised, if the House will permit me to vary the metaphor. £1 was demanded at the pistol's point. When it was given, £2 were demanded at the pistol's point. Finally the Dictator consented to take £1. 17s. 6d. and the rest in promises of goodwill for the future.

No one has been a more resolute and uncompromising struggler for peace than the Prime Minister. Everyone knows that. Never has there been such intense and undaunted determination to maintain and secure peace. Nevertheless, I am not quite clear why there was so much danger of Great Britain or France being involved in a war with Germany at this juncture if in fact they were ready all along to sacrifice Czechoslovakia. The terms which the Prime Minister brought back with him could easily have been agreed, I believe, through the ordinary diplomatic channels at any time during the summer. And I will say this, that I believe the Czechs, left to themselves, and told they were going to get no help from the Western Powers, would have been able to make better terms than they have got after all this tremendous perturbation. They could hardly have had worse.

All is over. Silent, mournful, abandoned, broken, Czechoslovakia recedes into the darkness. She has suffered in every respect by her associations with France, under whose guidance and policy she has been actuated for so long. . . .

I find unendurable the sense of our country falling into the power, into the orbit and influence of Nazi Germany, and of our existence becoming dependent upon their goodwill or pleasure. It is to prevent that that I have tried my best to urge the maintenance of every bulwark of defence —first, the timely creation of an Air Force superior to anything within striking distance of our shores; secondly, the gathering together of the collective strength of many nations; and, thirdly, the making of alliances and military conventions, all within the Covenant, in order to gather together forces at any rate to restrain the onward movement of this power. It has all been in vain. Every position has been successively undermined and abandoned on specious and plausible excuses.

I do not grudge our loyal, brave people, who were ready to do their duty no matter what the cost, who never flinched under the strain of last week, the natural, spontaneous outbursts of joy and relief when they learned that the hard ordeal would no longer be required of them at the moment; but they should know the truth. They should know that there has been gross neglect and deficiency in our defences; they should know that we have sustained a defeat without a war, the consequences of which will travel far with us along our road; they should know that we have passed an awful milestone in our history when the whole equilibrium of Europe has been deranged, and that the terrible words have for the time being been pronounced against the Western democracies: 'Thou art weighed in the balance and found wanting.' And do not suppose that this is the end. This is only the beginning of the reckoning. This is only the first sip, the first foretaste of a bitter cup which will be proffered to us year by year unless, by a supreme recovery of moral health and martial vigour, we arise again and take our stand for freedom as in the olden time.

(d) Germany and Poland, 1939

The British and French guarantee of independence, 31 March 1939. Neville Chamberlain's announcement in the House of Commons.

Source: W. S. Churchill, op. cit., p. 310.

I now have to inform the House that . . . in the event of any action which clearly threatened Polish independence and which the Polish Government accordingly considered it vital to resist with their national forces, His Majesty's Government would feel themselves bound at once to lend the Polish Government all support in their power. They have given the Polish Government an assurance to this effect.

I may add that the French Government have authorised me to make it plain that they stand in the same position in this matter as do His Majesty's Government. . . .

Hitler's communication to Sir Nevile Henderson, the British Ambassador, 25 August 1939. The Russo-German Non-Aggression Pact had been signed 23 August.

Source: N. Henderson, *Failure of a Mission* (1939), Appendix IV.

* * *

The Führer makes the following communication to the British Ambassador:

1. Poland's actual provocations have become intolerable. It makes no difference who is responsible. If the Polish Government denies responsibility, that only goes to show that it no longer itself possesses any influence over its

subordinate military authorities. In the preceding night there had been a further twenty-one new frontier incidents; on the German side the greatest discipline had been maintained. All incidents had been provoked from the Polish side. Furthermore, commercial aircraft had been shot at. If the Polish Government stated that it was not responsible, it showed that it was no longer capable of controlling its own people.

* * *

3. The problem of Danzig and the Corridor must be solved. The British Prime Minister had made a speech which was not in the least calculated to induce any change in the German attitude. At the most, the result of this speech could be a bloody and incalculable war between Germany and England. Such a war would be bloodier than that of 1914 to 1918. In contrast to the last war, Germany would no longer have to fight on two fronts. Agreement with Russia was unconditional and signified a change in foreign policy of the Reich which would last a very long time. Russia and Germany would never again take up arms against each other. Apart from this the agreements reached with Russia would also render Germany secure economically for the longest possible period of war.

The Führer had always wanted an Anglo-German understanding. War between England and Germany could at the best bring some profit to Germany but none at all to England.

The Führer declared that the German-Polish problem must be solved and will be solved. He is, however, prepared and determined after the solution of this problem to approach England once more with a large comprehensive offer. He is a man of great decisions, and in this case also he will be capable of being great in his action. He accepts the British Empire and is ready to pledge himself personally for its continued existence and to place the power of the German Reich at its disposal if—

(1) His colonial demands, which are limited and can be negotiated by peaceful methods, are fulfilled, and in this case he is prepared to fix the longest time limit.

(2) His obligations towards Italy are not touched; in other words, he does not demand that England gives up her obligations towards France, and similarly for his own part he cannot withdraw from his obligations towards Italy.

(3) He also desires to stress the irrevocable determination of Germany never again to enter into conflict with Russia. The Führer is ready to conclude agreements with England which, as has already been emphasised, would not only guarantee the existence of the British Empire in all circumstances as far as Germany is concerned, but also if necessary an assurance to the British Empire of German assistance regardless of where such assistance should be necessary. The Führer would then also be ready to accept a reasonable limitation of armaments which corresponds to the new political situation, and which is economically tolerable. Finally, the Führer renewed his assurances that he is not interested in Western problems and that a frontier modification in the West does not enter into consideration. Western fortifications which have been constructed at a cost of milliards were final Reich frontiers on the West.

If the British Government would consider these ideas a blessing for Germany and also for the British Empire would result. If it rejects these ideas there will be war. In no case would Great Britain emerge stronger; the last war proved this.

The Führer repeats that he is a man of ad infinitum decisions by which he himself is bound and that this is his last offer. Immediately after solution of the German-Polish question he would approach the British Government with an offer.

[TIMETABLE OF SUBSEQUENT EVENTS RELATING TO POLAND

This list should be related to the document above.

Source of quotation: N. Henderson, op. cit., p. 313.

28th August. British Government replied: they would stand by their guarantee to Poland, and proposed direct German-Polish negotiations.

29th August. Hitler replied, reasserting his case against Poland but 'for the rest, in making these proposals the German Government have never had any intention of touching Poland's vital interests or questioning the existence of an independent Polish State. The German Government, accordingly, in these circumstances agree to accept the British Government's offer of their good offices in securing the despatch to Berlin of a Polish Emissary with full powers. They count on the arrival of this Emissary on Wednesday, the 30th August, 1939.'

This implied the kind of surrender that Schuschnigg of Austria and Hacha of Czechoslovakia had had to make.

30th August. In an interview with Henderson, Ribbentrop read out, at high speed, the text of further German proposals, not submitted in writing until 9.15 p.m. 31st August, and never submitted to Poland, although the gist was conveyed to the Polish Ambassador by Henderson at 2 a.m. 31st August.

31st August, 12.30 (noon). Hitler signed First War Directive against Poland.

1st September, Dawn. German forces crossed Polish frontier.]

Austria

16. The Quadruple Alliance, 20 November 1815

Source: F. Martens, *Recueil des Traités et Conventions conclus par la Russie*, IV, 1, 28–34, in Butterfield, *Select Documents*, p. 101.

. . . Since the end of the alliance concluded in Vienna on the 25th March 1815 has been happily achieved by the re-establishment in France of the system which had been momentarily overturned during Napoleon Bonaparte's final bid for power, Their Majesties the Emperor of All the Russias, the King of . . . Great Britain . . . the Emperor of Austria . . . and the King of Prussia, considering that the peace of Europe is essentially bound up with the consolidation of that order of things, based as it is upon the maintenance of Royal authority and the retention of the Constitutional Charter; and wishing to use all their endeavours to prevent fresh disturbances from troubling the general tranquillity, which is the object of the prayers of mankind and the constant purpose of their strivings. . . .

Art. I. The High Contracting Parties reciprocally promise one another that they will maintain in its full force the treaty signed this day with His Most Christian Majesty (the King of France) and will take care that the stipulations of this treaty, as well as those of the special conventions connected with it, shall be strictly and faithfully carried out in all their extent.

* * *

VI. To ensure and facilitate the execution of the present treaty, and to consolidate the close relations which today unite the four Sovereigns for the good of the world, the High Contracting Parties have agreed to continue at stated times, either under the immediate auspices of their Sovereigns or through their respective ministers, the holding of conferences for the purpose of discussing the great common interests, and examining the measures which at each of these times will be judged the most salutary for the repose and prosperity of peoples and the maintenance of the peace of Europe.

17. The Carlsbad Decrees, 1819

Source: Meyer, *Corpus juris confoederationis Germanicae* (2nd ed.), II, 138 ff., in Robinson and Beard, p. 20.

1. A special representative of the ruler of each state shall be appointed for each university, with appropriate instructions and extended powers and shall reside in the place where the university is situated. This office may devolve upon the existing curator or upon any other individual whom the government may deem qualified.

The function of this agent shall be to see to the strictest enforcement of existing laws and disciplinary regulations; to observe carefully the spirit which is shown by the instructors in the university in their public lectures and regular courses, and, without directly interfering in scientific matters or in the methods of teaching, to give a salutary direction to the instruction, having in view the future attitude of the students. Lastly, he shall devote unceasing attention to everything that may promote morality, good order, and outward propriety among the students. . . .

2. The confederated governments mutually pledge themselves to remove from the universities or other public

educational institutions all teachers who, by obvious deviation from their duty, or by exceeding the limits of their functions, or by the abuse of their legitimate influence over the youthful minds, or by propagating harmful doctrines hostile to public order or subversive of existing governmental institutions, shall have unmistakably proved their unfitness for the important office entrusted to them. . . .

No teacher who shall have been removed in this manner shall be again appointed to a position in any public institution of learning in another state of the union.

3. Those laws which have for a long period been directed against secret and unauthorized societies in the universities shall be strictly enforced. . . .

* * *

[Press Law.]

1. So long as this decree shall remain in force no publication which appears in the form of daily issues, or as a serial not exceeding twenty sheets of printed matter, shall go to press in any state of the union without the previous knowledge and approval of the state officials.

* * *

6. The Diet shall have the right, moreover, to suppress on its own authority, without being petitioned, such writings included in Article 1, in whatever German state they may appear, as, in the opinion of a commission appointed by it, are inimical to the honour of the union, the safety of individual states, or the maintenance of peace and quiet in Germany. There shall be no appeal from such decisions, and the governments involved are bound to see that they are put into execution.

7. When a newspaper or periodical is suppressed by a decision of the Diet, the editor thereof may not within a

period of five years edit a similar publication in any state of the union.

[Investigating Committee.]

1. Within a fortnight, reckoned from the passage of this decree, there shall convene, under the auspices of the Confederation, in the city and federal fortress of Mayence, an extraordinary commission of investigation to consist of seven members, including the chairman.

2. The object of the commission shall be a joint investigation, as thorough and extensive as possible, of the facts relating to the origin and manifold ramifications of the revolutionary plots and demagogical associations directed against the existing constitution and the internal peace both of the union and of the individual states; . . .

18. The Congress of Troppau, December 1820

Metternich reviewed the achievements of the Congress in this circular.

Source: Metternich, *Mémoires*, III, 417–21, in Robinson and Beard, pp. 36–37.

The events which took place in Spain March 8 and at Naples July 2, as well as the catastrophe in Portugal, could not but arouse a feeling of the deepest indignation, apprehension, and sorrow in those who are called upon to guard the tranquillity of the nations; and, at the same time, it emphasized the necessity of uniting in order to determine in common the means of checking the misfortunes which threaten to envelop Europe. It was but natural that these sentiments should leave a deep impression upon those powers which had but lately stifled revolution and which now beheld it once more raise its head.

*　　*　　*

. . . The powers are exercising an incontestable right in taking common measures in respect to those States in which the overthrow of the government through a revolt, even if it be considered simply as a dangerous example, may result in a hostile attitude towards all constitutions and legitimate governments. The exercise of this right becomes an urgent necessity when those who have placed themselves in this situation seek to extend to their neighbours the ills which they have brought upon themselves and to promote revolt and confusion around them. . . .

Nothing could menace more directly the tranquillity of the neighbouring States than the revolution at Naples, gaining ground as it did daily. . . .

19. The Revolutions of 1848–49

(a) *Hungary.* The U.S.A. had shown great sympathy with the revolt, and Kossuth addressed this statement to the American people from his exile in Turkey.

Source: *Report of the Special Committee on the Reception of Governor Kossuth* (New York, 1852), in Robinson and Beard, pp. 103–7.

*   *   *

. . . I asked of the king not the complete independence of my beloved country—not even any new rights or privileges—but simply these three things:

1. That the inalienable rights, sanctioned by a thousand years and by the constitution of my fatherland, should be guaranteed by a national and responsible administration.

2. That every inhabitant of my country, without regarding language or religion, should be free and equal before the law—all classes having the same privileges and protection from the law.

3. That all the people of the Austrian empire that acknowledged the same person as emperor whom we

Hungarians recognized as king, and the same laws of succession, should have restored to them their ancient constitutional rights, of which they had been unjustly despoiled, modified to suit their wants and the spirit of the age.

The first demand was not for any new grant or concession, but simply a fresh guarantee. In the arrangement made with our ancestors, when, by their free will, they elevated the House of Hapsburg to the throne, a condition was made that the king should preserve the independence and constitution of the country. . . .

The second demand was still less for any political right. We asked for nothing more than a reform in the internal administration of the State,—a simple act of justice which the aristocracy owed the people; and in this how much the king would have gained! The strength of his throne would have been increased tenfold by thus winning the affections of his faithful people.

The third demand was prompted by humanity and fraternal feeling. It was the proper and holy mission of our nation as the oldest member of the empire, and possessing a constitutional form of government, to raise its voice in behalf of those sister nations under the same ruler, and that were united to us by so many ties of relationship. . . .

The king and royal family granted these requests, appealing to the sanctity of their oaths as a guarantee of their fulfilment; and I, weak in myself, but strong through the confidence of my countrymen and the noble sympathy of the Austrian people, proclaimed everywhere, amid the raging storm of revolution, that 'the house of Austria should stand; for by the blessing of the Almighty it had begun to move in the right direction, and would be just to its people'. It stood; and stood, too, at a time when, whatever might have been the fate of Hungary, the revolutionary tempest, under my direction, would have blown away this antiquated and helpless dynasty like chaff before the winds of heaven. . . .

On the very day they signed the grant of these moderate demands of the Hungarian people, and solemnly swore, before God and the nation to maintain them, they secretly resolved and planned the most cruel conspiracy against us. They determined to break their oaths, to desolate the land with insurrection, conflagration, and blood, till, feeble and exhausted under the burden of a thousand miseries, Hungary might be struck from the roll of living nations. Then they hoped by the power of the bayonet, and, if necessary, by the arms of Russia, to erect a united and consolidated empire, like the Russian, of sixteen various nations; they hoped to realize their long-conceived purpose of making themselves an absolute power. . . .

. . . Ten months we fought, and fought victoriously, in defence; and it was only when every attempt to bring about an honourable peace failed; when Francis Joseph, who was never our king, dared, in his manifesto of the 4th of March, 1849, to utter the curse 'that Hungary should exist no longer'; when there was no hope of arresting the Russian invasion by diplomacy; when we saw that we must fight to save ourselves from being struck off the earth as a nation; when the House of Austria, by its endless acts of injustice and cruelty, and by calling in the aid of a foreign power, had extinguished, in the heart of the Hungarian people, every spark of affection—then, and then only, after so much patience, the nation resolved to declare its absolute independence. Then the National Assembly spoke the words which had long been uttered by every patriotic tongue: 'Francis Joseph, thou beardless young Nero! Thou darest to say Hungary shall exist no more! We, the people, answer, we do and will exist; but you and your treacherous House shall stand no longer!

You shall no more be kings of Hungary! Be forever banished, ye perfidious traitors to the nation!' . . .

Oh, that Hungary had received but a slight token of moral support from the European powers,—from those powers whose dreams are troubled with fears of the advance of the Cossack. Had only an English or a French agent come to us during our struggle, what might he not have done! He too would have seen and estimated our ability to sustain ourselves; he would have observed the humanity, the love of order, the reverence for liberty, which characterized the Hungarian nation. Had these two powers permitted a few ships to come to Ossara, laden with arms for the noble patriots who had asked in vain for weapons, the Hungarians would now have stood a more impregnable barrier against Russia than all the arts of a miserable and expensive diplomacy.

* * *

. . . Before you I assert that the accusation that the Magyar race was unjust to the other races—by means of which a portion of the Servians, Wallachians, Slavonians, and Germans dwelling in Hungary was excited against us —is an impious slander, circulated by the House of Hapsburg, which shrinks from no crime to weaken the united forces of our united army, to conquer one race after another, and thus bring them all under the yoke of slavery.

It is true, some of the races in Hungary had reason to complain; but these subjects of complaint were the inevitable consequences of the pre-existing state of things and the Austrian interference. But the Croatians had no reason to complain. This race of half a million, in a separate province, had a national assembly of its own and enjoyed greater privileges than even the Hungarians. . . .

* * *

Louis Kossuth, Governor of Hungary.

THE REVOLUTIONS OF 1848-49

(b) *Petofi's Aspirations*. Alexander Petofi (1823–49) played a distinguished part in the revolt of 1848, and was killed in battle. His poetry expresses the Romantic's aspirations to Freedom and Nationhood. In this poem he castigates his countrymen for failing to rise to these.

Source: Sir John Bowring, *Translations from Alexander Petofi* (1866), p. 235, three verses have been omitted.

THE HUNGARIAN NATION

Is there in Magyar land a single spot
Unsanctified by hero Magyar blood?
Has not that blood which warmed our sires imbued
Our country's soil,—Alas! the scathing blot
Of shame is on their sons' ingratitude.

*   *   *

Has not this race of their forefathers heard?
Can the old blood run purely through their veins?
O if a drop of that old blood remains,
By some redeeming deed—some wakening word—
'Twill usher Freedom in and break our chains.

Why should we tarry? Are we humbled down
To very beasts of burden—satisfied
To eat the bread, by despot hands supplied—
Blanked in the records of the world's renown—
Than so to live, 'twere better to have died.

Shame on thee, outraged nation! Shame on thee.
Who once didst fill, in the heroic age
Of history's pages, a transcendent page,
And now thou kneelest in thine infamy,
A poor slave victim on the vulgar stage.

*   *   *

(c) *Russian Reactions*. The point of view put forward in this Russian proclamation should not be dismissed out of hand as simply a pretence.

Source: *The Annual Register*, 1849, p. 333.

The insurrection in Hungary has of late made so much progress that Russia cannot possibly remain inactive. . . .

The Magyar movement has been adulterated by the presence of Polish immigrants, forming whole corps of the Hungarian army . . . and they still keep the vast extent of our frontiers in a perpetual state of excitement and ferment. Such a state of things endangers our dearest interests. . . .

The Austrian government has formally requested His Majesty the Emperor to assist in the repression of a rebellion which endangers the tranquillity of the two empires.

Our safety is endangered by what is now doing and preparing in Hungary. . . . Any attack of theirs against the existence and the unity of the Austrian monarchy would also be an attack upon those territorial possessions which His Majesty deems necessary . . . for the equilibrium of Europe and the safety of his own States . . . the Emperor flatters himself that he acts in his own interests, and also in the interests of European peace and tranquillity.

20. The Ausgleich of 21 December 1867

Some of the provisions.

Source: *Annuaire de législation étrangère* (1875), IV, 259 ff., in Robinson and Beard, pp. 165–6.

Art. I. The following affairs are declared common to the realms and countries represented in the Reichsrath, and to the countries under the crown of Hungary:

(*a*) Foreign affairs, comprising the diplomatic and commercial representation in foreign countries as well as measures relating to international treaties, reserving the right of the ratification of the said treaties by the bodies representing each of the two halves of the empire (i.e. the Austrian Reichsrath and the Hungarian Reichstag), in so far as this approbation is constitutionally required.

(*b*) Military affairs, including the navy but excluding the determination of the quotas of troops and legislation regulating the Military service.

(*c*) Finances, relating to those expenses for which it is necessary to provide in common.

Art. II. The following matters are not to be treated in common, but are, from time to time, to be settled on the same basis by joint agreements.

1. Commercial matters, particularly tariff legislation.

2. Legislation on indirect taxes closely connected with industrial production.

3. The regulation of the monetary system and the system of coinage.

4. Arrangements affecting railway lines which concern both portions of the empire.

5. The establishment of a system of defence for the country.

Art. III. The common expenses are to be met by the two parts of the monarchy according to a ratio fixed by periodical agreements between the respective parliaments of the two parts of the empire, and approved by the emperor. The ways and means of raising the portion charged to each of the two parts of the empire remain the exclusive affair of each.

*   *   *

Art. V. The administration of the common affairs shall be vested in a joint responsible ministry, which is prohibited from managing, during the same period, the affairs peculiar to either of the two parts of the empire.

Arrangements concerning the management, conduct, and internal organization of the entire army belong exclusively to the emperor.

Art. VI. The parliaments of the two portions of the empire [the Austrian Reichsrath and the Hungarian Reichstag] shall exercise their legislative powers, which relate to common matters, through Delegations.

*   *   *

21. The Dual Alliance, 7 October 1879

The precise, military, secret commitments should be compared with the loose structure of the later Ententes and the first of Wilson's 14 points.

Source: G. F. von Martens, *Nouveau Recueil général de traités*, in Mowat, *Select Treaties and Documents*, p. 20.

Considering that Their Majesties the German Emperor, King of Prussia, and the Emperor of Austria, King of Hungary, must esteem it as their incontestable duty as sovereigns to take care in all circumstances for the security of their empires and for the tranquillity of their peoples;

Considering that the two monarchs as in the previously existing confederation will be in a position, by a firm alliance of the two empires, to fulfil this duty more easily and more efficaciously;

Considering, finally, that an intimate accord between Germany and Austria-Hungary can menace nobody, but is, on the contrary, qualified to consolidate the peace of Europe created by the stipulations of the Treaty of Berlin;

Their Majesties the German Emperor and the Emperor of Austria, King of Hungary, promising one another never to give any aggressive tendency in any direction to their purely defensive agreement, have resolved to conclude an alliance of peace and reciprocal protection.

* * *

Article I. If, contrary to expectation and against the sincere desire of both the High Contracting Parties, one of the two Empires shall be attacked on the part of Russia, the High Contracting Parties are bound to assist each other with the whole of the military power of their Empire, and consequently only to conclude peace conjointly and by agreement.

Article II. Should one of the High Contracting Parties be attacked by another Power, the other High Contracting Party hereby engages not only not to assist the aggressor against his High Ally, but at the least to observe a benevolent neutral attitude with regard to the High Contracting Party.

If, however, in such a case the attacking Power should be supported on the part of Russia, whether by way of active co-operation, or by military measures which menace the attacked Power, then the obligation of reciprocal assistance with full military power, which is stipulated in the first article of this Treaty will in this case enter immediately into effect, and the conduct of war of both the High Contracting Parties shall be then also in common until the joint conclusion of Peace.

Article III. This Treaty, in conformity with its pacific character and to prevent any misconstruction, shall be kept secret by both High Contracting Parties, and it will be communicated to a Third Power only with the consent of both Parties, and strictly according to a special agreement.

* * *

22. The annexation of Bosnia and Herzegovina by Austria, 7 October 1908

This is the Austrian point of view, and not at all how Serbia, Russia and Turkey saw it. The claims made for Austrian administration are substantially true.

Source: *The Weekly Times*, October 1908, in Robinson and Beard, pp. 401–3.

We, Francis Joseph, Emperor of Austria, King of Bohemia, and Apostolic King of Hungary, to the inhabitants of Bosnia and Herzegovina:

When a generation ago our troops crossed the borders of your lands, you were assured that they came not as foes, but as friends, with the firm determination to remedy the evils from which your fatherland had suffered so grievously for many years. This promise given at a serious moment has been honestly kept. It has been the constant endeavour of our government to guide the country by patient and systematic activity to a happier future.

*   *   *

. . . remembering the ties that existed of yore between our glorious ancestors on the Hungarian throne and these lands, we extend our suzerainty over Bosnia and Herzegovina, and it is our will that the order of succession of our House be extended to these lands also. The inhabitants of the two lands thus share all the benefits which a lasting confirmation of the present relation can offer. The new order of things will be a guarantee that civilization and prosperity will find a sure footing in your home.

Inhabitants of Bosnia and Herzegovina:

Among the many cares of our throne, solicitude for your material and spiritual welfare shall not be the last. The exalted idea of equal rights for all before the law, a share in the legislation and administration of the provincial affairs, equal protection for all religious creeds, languages, and racial differences, all these high possessions you shall enjoy in full measure.

The freedom of the individual and the welfare of the whole will be the aim of our government in the two lands. You will surely show yourselves worthy of the trust placed in you, by attachment and loyalty to us and to our House. And thus we hope that the noble harmony between the prince and the people, that dearest pledge of all social progress, will ever accompany us on our common path.

23. The Assassination of Archduke Franz Ferdinand, 28 June 1914

Source: *The Times*, Monday, 29 June 1914.

AUSTRIAN HEIR SHOT. DOUBLE ASSASSINATION. BOMBS AND BULLETS IN SARAJEVO.

Sarajevo, June 28th. 9.30 p.m.

Today at 9.50 a.m. the Imperial train conveying the Archduke Franz Ferdinand and his consort arrived here from Ilidza. After inspecting the troops on the Filipovitch parade ground the august visitors drove in a motor car along the station road and the Appel Quay to the Town Hall.

The first attempt, when the bomb was thrown, took place at 10.15, as the car was driving along the Appel Quay, just before reaching the Chumuria Bridge. An Aide de Campe seated in one of the motor cars was wounded in the neck by fragments of the bomb. The perpetrator was arrested. He is a young printer, 20 years of age, Nedjeliko Gabrinovitch by name, and a native of Herzegovina, belonging to the Serb Orthodox faith.

When the motor car conveying them reached the Town Hall, His Imperial Highness said to the Mayor 'What is the good of your speeches? I come to Sarajevo on a visit and I get bombs thrown at one. It is outrageous.'

When the procession drove back from the Town Hall, the second attempt was made. At 10.40, as the Heir Apparents' motor car reached the corner of the Appel Quay and of the Franz-Josefgasse, another bomb was thrown at the car by Savrilo Prinzip, a Bosnian High School student, also belonging to the Serb Orthodox faith. This bomb did not explode. Thereupon the assassin fired three shots from a revolver. The first shot hit the Archduke in the neck, the second hit him in the leg, and the third hit the Duchess of Hohenberg in the lower part of the body. . . .

The perpetrator was seized by the crowd and severely mauled. The Archduke and the Duchess of Hohenberg were rapidly conveyed to General Potiorek's official residence. Both were past all human aid and received the last sacrament. The Archduke expired a few moments after his Consort.

24. Ultimatum to Serbia, 6 p.m., 23 July 1914

Article No. 5 was not accepted outright by the Serbian Government, and this provided the pretext for war.

Source: *Collected Diplomatic Documents relating to the Outbreak of the European War* (London, 1915), in Butterfield, p. 191.

. . .The Royal Serbian Government shall publish on the front page of their 'Official Journal' of the 13th/26th July the following declaration:

'The Royal Government of Serbia condemn the propaganda that is being directed against Austria-Hungary,—

that is to say, condemn that group of tendencies which aim ultimately at the separation from the Austro-Hungarian monarchy of territories belonging to it. Also they sincerely deplore the fatal consequences of these criminal proceedings.

'The Royal Government regret that Serbian officers and functionaries have participated in the above-mentioned propaganda and have thus compromised the relations of good neighbourliness to which the Royal Government were solemnly pledged by their declaration of the 31st March, 1901. . . .'

This declaration shall be communicated to the Royal Army at the same time, as an order of the day, by H.M. the King and shall be published in the Official Bulletin of the Army.

* * *

The Royal Serbian Government shall further undertake:

1. To suppress any publication which incites to hatred and contempt of the [Austro-Hungarian] Monarchy and in its general bearing is directed against the territorial integrity of that monarchy;

2. To dissolve immediately the society called 'Narodna Odbrana', to confiscate all its means of propaganda, and to proceed in the same manner against the other societies and their branches in Serbia which devote themselves to propaganda against the Austro-Hungarian Monarchy. The Royal Government shall take the necessary measures to prevent the societies from continuing their activity under another name and form after they have been dissolved;

3. To eliminate without delay from public instruction in Serbia, both as regards the teaching body and also as regards the methods of instruction, everything which serves or might serve to foment the propaganda against Austria-Hungary;

4. To remove from the military service and from the administration in general, all officers and functionaries guilty of propaganda against the Austro-Hungarian Monarchy, whose names and deeds the Austro-Hungarian Government reserve to themselves the right of communicating to the Royal Government;

5. To accept the collaboration in Serbia of representatives of the Austro-Hungarian Government for the purpose of suppressing the subversive movement directed against the territorial integrity of the Monarchy;

6. To take judicial proceedings against those of the accessories to the plot of the 28th June who are within Serbian territory;

Delegates of the Imperial and Royal Government will take part in the investigation relating thereto;

* * *

9. To give explanations to the Imperial and Royal Government with regard to the unjustifiable utterances of high Serbian officials both in Serbia and abroad, who, notwithstanding their official position, have not hesitated in interviews since the crime of the 28th June to express themselves in a manner hostile to the Austro-Hungarian Monarchy; finally,

10. To notify the Imperial and Royal Government without delay of the execution of the measures comprised under the preceding heads.

The Austro-Hungarian Government expect the reply of the Royal Government by 6 p.m. on Saturday the 25th July at latest. . . .

25. The murder of Dollfuss, 1934

Source: *The Times*, Thursday, 26 July 1934 (condensed).

From our own correspondent.

Vienna, July 25th.

The Nazis carried out a most audacious putsch today in the heart of Vienna.

Clad in the uniforms of police, soldiers or auxiliaries, they went about 1 p.m. in four motor-lorries to the Federal Chancery, entered the courtyard and held Herr Dollfuss, the Chancellor and Major Fey the State Commissioner-General for extraordinary measures of security, prisoners. Another group forced its way about the same time into the Headquarters of the Austrian Broadcasting Company in the Inner City and terrorized the officials. One of the conspirators then went to the microphone and announced to Austria and the world that Herr Dollfuss had resigned in favour of Herr Rintelen, the Austrian Minister in Rome, who is now in Vienna. Action was at once begun and there was sharp fighting with machine guns and small arms.

The rest of the Cabinet met in the Ministry of War. They were reported to have informed the insurgents in the Chancery, which was surrounded by police and auxiliaries, that they must surrender by 4 p.m.

Soon after 4.30, Major Fey appeared at a window and informed the commander of the Police detachment that the Chancellor was seriously wounded and, desiring to spare the country further bloodshed, had resigned.

According to information received in London, Herr Dollfuss told the Nazis 'You can do with me what you like, I am going out of the building now. If you want to shoot me, then I shall die for my Fatherland.' Three Nazis then shot him.

Source: *The Times*, 26 July 1934.

Rome, July 26th.

An Official Statement.

From the first announcement of the assassination of Chancellor Dollfuss, that is to say at 4 p.m. on July 25th, to guard against eventual complications, orders were given for the movement of armed troops of the Army and Air Force towards the frontiers of the Brenner and of Carinthia.

26. The Anschluss, 1938

Source: *The Times*, Monday, 14 March 1938 (condensed).

THE FUHRER ENTERS HIS HOMELAND

Vienna, March 13th.

Herr Hitler returned yesterday, a conquering hero, to the land he left some twenty five years ago—an embittered young man passionately convinced that the only hope for Austria lay in union with the Reich. . . .

This triumphant welcome was shared by the army he had sent into Austria; flowers were strewn in the path of the rumbling tractors and armoured cars. If any Austrians were against him on Friday, they either hid their faces or were completely converted yesterday and today. . . .

Herr Hitler crossed the Austrian frontier yesterday afternoon at 3.50 at a spot near his birthplace, Branau. At 4 o'clock he reached Branau, which was in a state of frantic excitement and spent 20 minutes there, visiting the house where he was born. His arrival in Linz, which had never seen such crowds, was unforgettable. Standing in the great open car which could scarcely make its way through the masses of people, he repeatedly acknowledged the welcome of his countrymen.

Dr. von Seyss-Inquart, in greeting him, said:

'In spite of a dictated peace treaty, Germans have found their way to each other. Today the entire German people stand united and indivisible. . . . You, my Fuhrer, are the Leader of the German nation in its struggle for honour, freedom and right. . . .'

While Herr Hitler was speaking (in reply) the march of the German Forces—motor cyclists, armoured cars, motor machine guns, anti-tank guns and the like—continued all over Austria. One of the most picturesque and historically interesting incidents was the encounter with Italian troops when the Brenner pass was reached.

The German commander advanced to the Italian post and said:

'I have orders to proceed with a small part of my Forces to the Italian fronter. Movements are being carried out in a completely friendly feeling and in the spirit which corresponds to the friendly relations between National Socialist Germany and Fascist Italy.' . . .

During the day Herr Hitler sent the following telegram to Rome:

'Mussolini—Ich werde Ihnen dieses nie vergessen.'

The literal meaning is 'I shall never forget you for this'.

The British Government reacted to the Anschluss as shown in this statement of Neville Chamberlain, reported in *The Times* on 15 March:

Throughout these events, H.M. Government have remained in the closest touch with the French Government, and the French Government have also entered a strong protest in Berlin on similar lines to that lodged by H.M. Government.

It seems to us that the methods adopted call for the severest condemnation and have administered a profound shock to all who are interested in the preservation of

European peace. It follows that what has passed cannot fail to have prejudiced the hope . . . of removing misunderstandings between nations and promoting international co-operation.

. . . There is, of course, no foundation for any of these rumours [that the Government had consented or even encouraged the absorption of Austria].

As regards our defence programmes, we have always made it clear that they were flexible and that they would have to be reviewed from time to time in the light of any development in the international situation. It would be idle to pretend that recent events do not constitute a change of the kind we had in mind. Accordingly, we have decided to make a fresh review, and in due course we shall announce what further steps we think it necessary to take.

Russia

27. The Early Liberalism of Tsar Alexander I

The Polish Prince Adam Czartoryski (1770–1861) knew Alexander before he became Tsar.

Source: *Memoirs of Prince Adam Czartoryski*, I, in Robinson and Beard, p. 338.

As soon as I came in the Grand Duke Alexander took me by the hand and proposed that we should go into the garden. We walked about in every direction for three hours, keeping up an animated conversation all the time. He declared that he did not in any way share the ideas and doctrines of the cabinet and the court; and that he was far from approving the policy and conduct of his grandmother, whose principles he condemned. He had wished for the success of Poland in her glorious struggle and had deplored her fall. Kosciuszko, he said, was, in his eyes, a man who was great by his virtues as well as owing to the cause which he had defended,—the cause of humanity and justice. He added that he detested despotism everywhere, no matter in what way it was exercised; that he loved liberty, to which all men had a right; that he had taken the strongest interest in the French Revolution, and that while condemning its terrible excesses, he wished the French Republic success and rejoiced at its establishment.

I was deeply moved, and could hardly believe my ears. That a Russian prince, Catherine II's successor, her grandson and her favourite child, whom she would have wished to see reigning after her instead of her son, and of whom it was said that he would continue her reign, should disavow and detest his grandmother's principles, should repel the odious policy of Russia, should be a passionate lover of justice and liberty, should pity Poland and wish to see her happy,—all this seemed incredible. And that such noble ideas and great virtues should be able to grow and flourish in such an atmosphere and with such surroundings was surely little less than a miracle.

It should be remembered that at that time so-called liberal opinions were much less prevalent than they are now, and had not yet penetrated into all the classes of society or even into the cabinets of sovereigns. On the contrary, everything that had the appearance of liberalism was anathematized in the courts and salons of most of the European capitals, and especially in Russia and at St. Petersburg, where all the convictions of the old French régime were grafted in an exaggerated form on Russian despotism and servility.

28. Serfdom

Prince Kropotkin joined the revolutionary movement in 1872, escaped to the West, returning to Moscow after the February Revolution of 1917. An anarchist and anti-Marxist, he opposed state and private property alike.

Source: Kropotkin, *Memoirs of a Revolutionist* (1899) (condensed) in Robinson and Beard, pp. 345–6.

Wealth was measured in those times by the number of 'souls' that a landed proprietor owned. So many 'souls' meant so many male serfs; women did not count. My father, who owned nearly twelve hundred souls, in three different provinces, and who had, in addition to his peasants' holdings, large tracts of land which were cultivated by these peasants, was accounted a rich man. He lived up to his reputation, which meant that his house was open to any number of visitors, and that he kept a very large household.

We were a family of eight, occasionally of ten or twelve; but fifty servants at Moscow and half as many more in the country were considered not one too many. Four coachmen to attend a dozen horses, three cooks for the masters and two more for the servants, a dozen men to wait upon us at dinner time (one man, plate in hand, standing behind each person seated at the table), and girls innumerable in the maidservants' room,—how could any one do with less than this? Besides, the ambition of every landed proprietor was that everything required for his household should be made at home, by his own men.

To maintain such numbers of servants as were kept in our house in town would have been simply ruinous, if all provisions had to be bought at Moscow; but in those times of serfdom things were managed very simply. When winter came, father sat at his table and wrote the following to the manager of his estate:

'On receipt of this, and as soon as winter communication is established in the city of Moscow, twenty-five peasant sledges, drawn by two horses each, one horse from each house, and one sledge and one man from each second house, are to be loaded with (so many) quarters of oats, (so many) of wheat, and (so many) of rye, as also with all the poultry and geese and ducks, well frozen, which have to be killed this winter, well packed and accompanied by a complete list, under the supervision of a well-chosen man'; —and so it went on for a couple of pages, till the next full stop was reached. After this there followed an enumeration of the penalties which would be inflicted in case the provisions should not reach the house situated in such a street, number so and so, in due time and in good condition.

Some time before Christmas the twenty-five peasant sledges really entered our gates, and covered the surface of the wide yard. . . .

29. The Edict of Emancipation, 3 March 1861

These are some of its main provisions (condensed).
Source: *Annual Register* of 1861.

We, Alexander II, by the grace of God Tsar and Autocrat of all the Russias, King of Poland, Grand Duke of Finland, etc., make known to all our faithful subjects:

* . *   *

The peasants now bound to the soil shall, within the term fixed by the law, be vested with the full rights of freemen. The landed proprietors, while they shall retain all the rights of ownership over all the lands now belonging to them, shall transfer to the peasants, in return for a rent fixed by law, the full enjoyment of their cottages, farm buildings, and gardens. Furthermore, in order to assure to the peasants their subsistence and enable them to meet their obligations towards the State, the landlords shall turn over to the peasants a quantity of arable and other land provided for in the regulations above mentioned. In return for these allotments the peasant families shall be required to pay rent to the landlords, as fixed by the provisions of the law. Under these conditions, which are temporary, the peasants shall be designated as 'temporarily bound'.

At the same time the peasants are granted the right of purchasing their cottages and gardens, and, with the consent of the landlords, they may acquire in complete ownership the arable lands and other lands allotted to them as a permanent holding. By the acquisition of a complete title to the land assigned them, the peasants[7] shall be freed from their obligations toward the landlords for land thus purchased, and thus enter definitively into the class of free peasants and landowners.

* * *

Aware of all the difficulties of the reform we have undertaken, we place our trust in the goodness of Divine Providence, who watches over the destinies of Russia. We also count upon the generous devotion of our faithful nobility, and we are happy to testify to that body the gratitude it has deserved from us, as well as from the country, for the disinterested support it has given to the accomplishment of our designs. Russia will not forget that the nobility, actuated solely by its respect for the dignity of man and its love for its neighbour, has spontaneously renounced the rights it enjoyed in virtue of the system of serfdom now abolished, and has laid the foundation of a new future for the peasants. We also entertain the firm hope that it will also direct its further efforts to carry out the new regulation by maintaining good order, in a spirit of peace and benevolence.

In order to render the transactions between the landlords and the peasants easier, so that the latter may acquire in full proprietorship their houses and the adjacent lands and buildings, the government will grant them assistance, according to a special regulation, through loans of money or a transfer of mortgages encumbering an estate.

* * *

And now we confidently hope that the freed serfs, in the presence of the new future which is opened before them, will appreciate and recognize the considerable sacrifices which the nobility has made on their behalf. . . .

[7] This does not mean the individual peasants, but the village community, which was perpetuated under the new law.

. . . Only by assiduous labour, a rational expenditure of their strength and resources, a strict economy, and, above all, by an upright life,—a life constantly inspired by the fear of the Lord,—can they hope for prosperity and progress.

And now, my orthodox and faithful people, make the holy sign of the cross and join thy prayers to ours, invoking the blessing of the Most High upon thy first free labours, for this alone is a sure pledge of private well-being and the public weal.

Given at St. Petersburg, the nineteenth day of February[8] of the year of grace 1861 and the seventh of our reign.

Alexander

30. Peasant and Landowner after Emancipation

In some ways the Edict of Emancipation made the lot of the peasants even more arduous and precarious.

Leo Tolstoy (1828–1910) was the great novelist who wrote *War and Peace* (1863–69). Of aristocratic family, he fought at Sebastopol as an artillery officer.

Source: Leo Tolstoy, *What Then Must We Do?* (1886), tr. Aylmer Maude, pp. 199–204 (condensed).

The work is intense and ceaseless. All work with their utmost strength and during this work eat up not only all their scanty supplies of food but also any reserves they may have had: never too stout, they grow leaner by the end of the harvest work.

Here is a small group engaged on mowing: three peasants—one an old man, another his nephew (a young married lad), and a boot-maker, a sinewy fellow who has been a domestic serf—this hay-harvest decides their fate for the coming winter for them all: whether they can keep

[8] Old style calendar.

a cow and pay the taxes. They have already worked unceasingly and continuously for two weeks. Rain has hindered the work. After the rain, when the wind has dried the grass, they decide to finish the work, and to get on more quickly they decide each to bring two women to it. With the old man comes his wife, a woman of fifty worn out by hard work and eleven childbirths, and deaf but still a good worker, and his thirteen-year-old daughter, a small girl but strong and quick. With the nephew comes his wife, a woman as strong and tall as a man, and his sister-in-law the pregnant wife of a soldier. With the bootmaker comes his wife, a good worker, and her mother, an old woman finishing her eighth decade and who usually goes out begging. They all line up, and work from morning till evening in the sweltering blaze of the June sun. It is steaming and the rain threatens. Every hour of work is precious. They grudge the time to fetch water or kvas.

A tiny boy, the old woman's grandson, fetches some water for them. The old woman, evidently only anxious not to be driven away from the work, does not let the rake out of her hands, though she can hardly, with effort, move along. The lad, all bent up and taking short steps with his bare little feet, brings along the jug of water which is heavier than himself, changing it from hand to hand. The girl shoulders a load of hay which is also heavier than she; she takes a few steps, stops, and throws it down unable to carry it farther. The old woman of fifty rakes unceasingly and, with her kerchief brushed to one side, drags the hay along, breathing heavily and tottering in her walk; the woman of eighty does nothing but rake, but even that is beyond her strength; she slowly drags her feet in their bark shoes, and with wrinkled brows looks sombrely before her like one who is seriously ill or is dying. The old man purposely sends her farther away from the others to rake near the hay-cocks so that she should not have to keep up with them, but without pause and with the same death-like, sombre face she works on as long as the others do.

The sun is already setting behind the woods and the hay-cocks are not yet all cleared away and much remains to be done. . . .

But here is the proprietor's house. That same evening when from the village is heard the clang of the whetstones of the exhausted hay-makers returning from the fields, the sounds of the hammers straightening out the dents in the scythe blades, the shouts of women and girls who, having just had time to put down their rakes, are already running to drive in the cattle—from the proprietor's house other sounds are heard: drin, drin, drin! goes the piano, and an Hungarian song rings out, and amid those songs occasionally comes the sound of the knock of croquet-mallets on the balls. Near the stable stands a carriage to which four well-fed horses are harnessed. It is a smart hired carriage. . . .

* * *

In that house two women hardly manage to wash up all the crockery for the gentlefolk who have just had a meal, and two peasants in dress coats are running up and down stairs serving coffee, tea, wine, and seltzer water. Upstairs a table is spread: they have just finished eating and will soon eat again till midnight, till three o'clock, often till cock-crow.

Some of them sit smoking and playing cards, others sit and smoke talking liberalism; others move about from place to place, eat, smoke, and not knowing what to do decide to go out for a drive. There are some fifteen healthy men and women there and some thirty able-bodied men and women servants working for them.

* * *

Here it is no longer possible to make the excuse that such is the order of things; none of it was prearranged. We ourselves carefully arrange this way of life, taking grain and labour away from the overburdened peasant folk. We live as though we had no connection with the dying washer-woman, the fifteen-year-old prostitute, the woman fagged out by cigarette-making, and the strained, excessive labour of the old women and children around us who lack a sufficiency of food; we live—enjoying ourselves in luxury—as if there were no connection between those things and our life; we do not wish to see that were it not for our idle, luxurious and depraved way of life, there would also not be this excessive toil, and that without this excessive toil such lives as ours would be impossible.

We imagine that their sufferings are one thing and our life another, and that we, living as we do, are as innocent and pure as doves.

31. A Political Prisoner in Siberia

Source: Leo Deutsch, *Sixteen Years in Siberia* (1905) (condensed), pp. 95–97, 115.

A fortnight after my arrest I was informed that a party of convicts would start for Moscow that evening. I was to accompany them, and accordingly must assume the convict garb. After eighteen years I think of that day with a shudder.

First of all, I was taken into a room where was stored everything necessary to the equipment of a convict under sentence. On the floor lay piles of chains; and clothes, boots, etc., were heaped on shelves. From among them some were selected that were supposed to fit me; and I was then conducted to a second room. Here the right side of my head was shaved, and the hair on the left side cut short.

I had seen people in the prison who had been treated in this fashion, and the sight had always made a painful impression on me, as indeed it does on every one. But when I saw my own face in the glass a cold shudder ran down my spine, and I experienced a sensation of personal degradation to something less than human. I thought of the days—in Russia not so long ago—when criminals were branded with hot irons. A convict was waiting ready to fasten on my fetters. I was placed on a stool, and had to put my foot on an anvil. The blacksmith fitted an iron ring round each ankle, and welded it together. Every stroke of the hammer made my heart sink, as I realised that a new existence was beginning for me.

The mental depression into which I now fell was soon accompanied by physical discomfort. The fetters at first caused me intolerable pain in walking, and even disturbed my sleep. It also required considerable practice before one can easily manage to dress and undress. The heavy chains, about thirteen pounds in weight, are not only an encumbrance, but are very painful, as they chafe the skin round the ankles; and the leather lining is but little protection to those unaccustomed to these adornments. Another great torment is the continual clinking of the chains. It is indescribably irritating to the nervous, and reminds the prisoner at every turn that he is 'deprived of all rights'. I hardly knew myself as I looked in the glass and beheld a fully attired convict. . . .

We were taken straight to the railway carriage engaged for us by the organizers of the convoy. I asked my companions the reason of their banishment, and learned from them that—as in many other instances described to me by people who had similarly been exiled to Siberia—they had simply been accused by the police of being 'untrustworthy'. This word has become classical in Russian police affairs, and has a conveniently vague signification.

Literally it means 'of whom nothing good can be expected'. A young man or girl associates with so-and-so, reads such and such books; this is enough to awaken suspicion that the said young man or girl is 'untrustworthy'. The police or the gendarmerie pay a domiciliary visit, find a suspicious letter or a prohibited book, and then the course of events is certain,—arrest, imprisonment, Siberia. It may be scarcely credible that people languish for years in prison, without any pretence of legal procedure against them, simply by decree of an officer of the gendarmerie; and that at the good pleasure of these officers—most of them fabulously ignorant men—people are banished to the wilds of Siberia. Even those familiar with Russian affairs are often shocked and staggered by some fresh case of this kind.

32. The Unrest Accompanying the Russo-Japanese War, 1904–5

(a) Bloody Sunday, 22 January 1905

Source: *The Weekly Times*, 27 January 1905, in Robinson and Beard, pp. 373–8 (condensed).

A more perfect and lovely day never dawned. The air was crisp and the sky almost cloudless. The gilded domes of the cathedrals and churches, brilliantly illuminated by the sun, formed a superb panorama. I noticed a significant change in the bearing of the passers-by. They were all wending their way, singly or in small groups, in the direction of the Winter Palace. Joining in the stream of workingmen, I proceeded in the direction of the Winter Palace. No observer could help being struck by the look of sullen determination on every face. Already a crowd of many thousands had collected, but was prevented from entering the square by mounted troops drawn up across the thoroughfare. Presently the masses began to press forward threateningly. The cavalry advanced at a walking pace, scattering the people right and left.

Event has succeeded event with such bewildering rapidity that the public is staggered and shocked beyond measure. The first trouble began at 11 o'clock, when the military tried to turn back some thousands of strikers at one of the bridges. The same thing happened almost simultaneously at other bridges, where the constant flow of workmen pressing forward refused to be denied access to the common rendezvous in the Palace Square. The Cossacks at first used their knouts, then the flat of their sabres, and finally they fired. The strikers in the front ranks fell on their knees and implored the Cossacks to let them pass, protesting that they had no hostile intentions. They refused, however, to be intimidated by blank cartridges, and orders were given to load with ball.

The passions of the mob broke loose like a bursting dam. The people, seeing the dead and dying carried away in all directions, the snow on the streets and pavements soaked with blood, cried aloud for vengeance. Meanwhile the situation at the Palace was becoming momentarily worse. The troops were reported to be unable to control the vast masses which were constantly surging forward. Reinforcements were sent and at 2 o'clock here also the order was given to fire. Men, women, and children fell at each volley, and were carried away in ambulances, sledges, and carts. The indignation and fury of every class were aroused. Students, merchants, all classes of the population alike were inflamed. At the moment of writing, firing is going on in every quarter of the city.

Father Gapon, marching at the head of a large body of workmen, carrying a cross and other religious emblems, was wounded in the arm and shoulder. The two forces of workmen are now separated. Those on the other side of the river are arming with swords, knives, and smiths' and carpenters' tools, and are busy erecting barricades. The troops are apparently reckless, firing right and left, with or without reason. The rioters continue to appeal to them, saying, 'You are Russians! Why play the part of blood-thirsty butchers?'

Dreadful anxiety prevails in every household where any members are absent. Distracted husbands, fathers, wives, and children are searching for those missing. The surgeons and Red Cross ambulances are busy. A night of terror is in prospect.

(b) Dissolution of the First Duma

The Tsar called a Duma (10 May 1906) in response to the widespread unrest, but dissolved it on 21 July 1906, issuing the following manifesto.

Source: op. cit., 27 July 1906.

We summoned the representatives of the nation by our will to the work of productive legislation. Confiding firmly in divine clemency and believing in the great and brilliant future of our people, we confidently anticipated benefits for the country from their labours. We proposed great reforms in all departments of the national life. We have always devoted our greatest care to the removal of the ignorance of the people by the light of instruction, and to the removal of their burdens by improving the conditions of agricultural work.

A cruel disappointment has befallen our expectations. The representatives of the nation, instead of applying themselves to the work of productive legislation, have strayed into spheres beyond their competence, and have been making inquiries into the acts of local authorities established by ourselves, and have been making comments upon the imperfections of the fundamental laws, which can only be modified by our imperial will. In short, the representatives of the nation have undertaken really illegal acts, such as the appeal by the Duma to the nation.

The peasants, disturbed by such anomalies, and seeing no hope of the amelioration of their lot, have resorted in a number of districts to open pillage and the destruction of other people's property, and to disobedience of the law and of the legal authorities. But our subjects ought to remember that an improvement in the lot of the people is only possible under conditions of perfect order and tranquillity. We shall not permit arbitrary or illegal acts, and we shall impose our imperial will on the disobedient by all the power of the State. . . .

*   *   *

In dissolving the Duma we confirm our immutable intention of maintaining this institution, and in conformity with this intention we fix March 5, 1907, as the date of the convocation of a new Duma by a ukase addressed to the Senate. With unshakable faith in divine clemency and in the good sense of the Russian people, we shall expect from the new Duma the realization of our efforts and their promotion of legislation in accordance with the requirements of a regenerated Russia.

Faithful sons of Russia, your Tsar calls upon you as a father upon his children to unite with him for the regeneration of our holy fatherland. We believe that giants in thought and action will appear, and that, thanks to their assiduous efforts, the glory of Russia will continue to shine.

Nicholas

33. The Russian Revolution, 1917

(a) The February Revolution, 23–27 February

Source: Leon Trotsky, *History of the Russian Revolution*, tr. Max Eastman, pp. 119–46 (condensed).

The 23rd of February was International Woman's Day. . . . It had not occurred to anyone that it might become the first day of the revolution. However, in spite of all directives, the women textile workers in several factories went on strike. . . .

Thus the fact is that the February Revolution was begun from below, the initiative being taken of their own accord by the most oppressed and downtrodden part of the proletariat—the women textile workers, among them no doubt many soldiers' wives. The overgrown bread lines had provided the last stimulus. About 90,000 workers, men and women, were on strike that day. . . . The movement began in the Vyborg district with its large industrial establishment, thence it crossed over to the Petersburg side. . . . A mass of women flocked to the municipal duma demanding bread. It was like demanding milk from a he-goat. Red banners appeared in different parts of the city, and inscriptions on them showed that the workers wanted bread, but neither autocracy nor war.

On the following day the movement doubles. The slogan 'Bread!' is crowded out or obscured by louder slogans 'Down with Autocracy'. But the Cossacks, constantly, though without ferocity, kept charging the crowd. There was no fear in the crowd. 'The Cossacks promised not to shoot' passed from mouth to mouth. And in fact they didn't. Towards the police the crowd showed ferocious hatred. They routed the mounted police with whistles, stones and pieces of ice.

It seems that the break in the army first appeared

amongst the Cossacks, those age-old subduers and punishers. On the 25th the strike spread wider. The soldiers show indifference, at times hostility to the police. A worker-Bolshevik, Kayurov, one of the authentic leaders in those days relates how, within sight of a detachment of Cossacks, the demonstrators scattered under the whips of the mounted police, and how he, Kayurov and several workers took off their caps and approached the Cossacks with the words 'Brothers—Cossacks, help the workers in their struggle for their peaceable demands; you see how the Pharaohs [9] treat us, hungry workers. Help us!'

'The Cossacks glanced at each other in some special way' continues Kayurov 'and we were hardly out of the way before they rushed into the fight.'

And a few minutes later, the crowd were tossing in their arms a Cossack who before their eyes had slaughtered a police inspector with his sabre.

February 27th: All the thoughts of the workers were concentrated on the army. The Vyborg section staged a meeting near the barracks of the Moscow regiment. The workers were scattered by a cruel fire. Officers with machine guns interfered between the workers and the soldiers. The answer was 'The soldiers have the firearms, go get them'. Either the machine gun will wipe out the insurrection, or the insurrection will capture the machine gun.

Only accidental fragments of what happened in those hours along the line of contact between workers and soldiers have come down to us.

The soldiers of the Volynsky regiment were the first to revolt. The training squad—that is the unit specially relied on to put down the insurrection—had refused to march out, its commander was killed. Having burned their bridges behind them, the Volynsky hastened to broaden

[9] Derisive nickname.

the base of the insurrection. They rushed into the neighbouring barracks, 'calling out' the soldiers, as strikers do.
The Moscow regiment joined the uprising, not without
inner struggle. The monarchist command impotently fell
away from the soldier mass, and either hid in the cracks or
hastened to change its colours. The Czarist garrison of
the capital, numbering 150,000 soldiers was dwindling,
melting, disappearing. By night it no longer existed.

Can it be that that was the whole resistance put up by
the redoubtable Russian Empire in the face of mortal
danger? Yes, that was about all—in spite of its great experience in crushing the people and its meticulously
elaborated plans. The monarchists explained the ease of
the February victory of the people by the peculiar
character of the Petrograd garrison. But the whole further
course of the revolution refutes this explanation. The
whole truth is that the fabric of the régime had completely
decayed; there was not a live thread left.

(b) Lenin's Arrival at the Finland Station, Petrograd, 16 April

This event has been seized upon by historians as one of the
focal points of the Revolution. Here it is described, with some
irony, by N. N. Sukhanov, an eye-witness and a member of
the Petrograd Soviet. Chkheidze was President of the Petrograd Soviet, and viewed the arrival of the Bolshevik leader with
apprehension.

Source: N. N. Sukhanov, *The Russian Revolution, 1917*. A
personal record edited and abridged by Joel Carmichael,
pp. 272–3.

. . . A thunderous Marseillaise boomed forth on the platform, and shouts of welcome rang out. We stayed in the
imperial waiting-rooms while the Bolshevik generals exchanged greetings. Then we heard them marching along
the platform, under the triumphal arches, to the sound of

the band, and between rows of welcoming troops and workers. The gloomy Chkheidze, the rest of us after him, got up, went to the middle of the room and prepared for the meeting. And what a meeting it was, worthy of—more than my wretched pen! . . .

Lenin came, or rather ran into the room. He wore a round cap, his face looked frozen, and there was a magnificent bouquet in his hands. Running to the middle of the room, he stopped in front of Chkheidze as though colliding with a completely unexpected obstacle. And Chkheidze, still glum, pronounced the following 'speech of welcome' with not only the spirit and wording but also the tone of a sermon:

'Comrade Lenin, in the name of the Petersburg Soviet and of the whole revolution we welcome you to Russia. . . . But—we think that the principal task of the revolutionary democracy is now the defence of the revolution from any encroachments either from within or without. We consider that what this goal requires is not disunion, but the closing of the democratic ranks. We hope you will pursue these goals together with us.'

[Lenin replied:]

. . . 'Dear comrades, soldiers, sailors and workers. I am happy to greet in your persons the victorious Russian revolution, and greet you as the vanguard of the world-wide proletarian army . . . the piratical imperialist war is the beginning of civil war throughout Europe . . . worldwide socialism has already dawned. . . . Germany is seething . . . any day now the whole of European capitalism may crash. The Russian revolution accomplished by you has prepared the way and opened a new epoch. Long live the world-wide socialist revolution.'

Suddenly, before the eyes of all of us, completely swallowed up by the routine drudgery of the revolution,

there was presented a bright, blinding, exotic beacon. . . .
Lenin's voice, heard straight from the train, was a 'voice
from outside'. There had broken in upon us in the revolution a note that was . . . novel, harsh and somewhat
deafening. . . .

(c) The Bolshevik Revolution: Lenin's Cry for Action

Letter to the Central Committee, the Petrograd and Moscow
Committees of the Russian Social Democratic Labour Party,
written 25–27 September 1917.

Source: Lenin, *Toward the Seizure of Power*, I, pp. 221–3,
  Edition Olgin and Tractenberg.

Having obtained a majority in the Soviets of Workers' and
Soldiers' deputies of both capitals, the Bolsheviks can and
must take power into their own hands.

They can do so because the active majority of the revolutionary elements of the people of both capitals is
sufficient to attract the masses, to overcome the resistance
of the adversary, to vanquish him, to conquer power and
to retain it. For, in offering immediately a democratic
peace, in giving the land immediately to the peasants, in
re-establishing the democratic institutions and liberties
which have been mangled and crushed by Kerensky, the
Bolsheviks will form a government which *nobody* will overthrow.

* * *

The Democratic Conference[10] does not represent the
majority of the revolutionary people, but only the con-
ciliatory petty-bourgeois top layer. The Democratic Conference deceives the peasantry without giving it either
peace or land. The Bolshevik government *alone* will
satisfy the peasantry.

What we are concerned with is not the day of the up-

[10] Called by Kerensky to try to widen support for his government.

rising, not the moment of the uprising in the narrow sense of the word. This will be decided by the common voice of those who are in contact with the workers and soldiers, with the masses.

What matters is that we must make the task clear to the party, place on the order of the day the *armed uprising* in Petrograd and Moscow (including their regions) the conquest of power, the overthrow of the government. We must think of *how* to make propaganda in favour of this, without committing ourselves in the press. We must recall and ponder the words of Marx on uprising—'Uprising is an art' etc.

It would be naive to wait for a formal majority on the side of the Bolsheviks; no revolution ever waits for this. Kerensky and Co. are not waiting either. . . . It is just the miserable vacillations of the Democratic Conference that must and will cause the patience of the workers of Petrograd and Moscow to end in a violent outburst. History will not forgive us if we do not assume power now.

No apparatus? There is an apparatus. The Soviets and democratic organisations. The international situation just now, on the eve of a separate peace between the English and the Germans, is in our favour.

Assume power at once in Moscow and in Petrograd (it does not matter which begins; perhaps even Moscow may begin); we will win absolutely and unquestionably.

N. Lenin.

(d) The Bolshevik Revolution: Proclamation and Appeals

Source: *Novaia Zhizn*, 8 November and *Izvestiia*, 8 November, in Bunyan and Fisher, *The Bolshevik Revolution*, pp. 100–1.

Proclamation of the Military Revolutionary Committee,

10.00 a.m., 7 November.

The Provisional Government is deposed. All state authority has passed into the hands of the Military Revolutionary Committee, the organ of the Petrograd Soviet of Workers' and Soldiers' Deputies acting in the name of the Petrograd proletariat and the garrison.

The causes for which the people were struggling—immediate democratic peace, abolition of the pomeschik's (landlord) right to the land, labour control of industry, and a Soviet form of government—are now all guaranteed.

Long live the revolution of Workers, Soldiers and Peasants!

Appeals of the Provisional Government.

November 7th

To the People

Citizens! Save the fatherland, the republic, and freedom! Maniacs have raised a revolt against the only governmental power chosen by the people—the Provisional Government.

The members of the provisional Government, faithful to duty, will remain at their posts and continue to work for the good of the fatherland, the re-establishment of order, and the convocation of the Constituent Assembly, the future sovereign of Russia and of the peoples inhabiting it.

Citizens, you must help the Provisional Government. You must strengthen its authority. You must oppose these maniacs, with whom are joined all enemies of liberty and order including the followers of the old régime whose purpose is to destroy all conquests of the revolution and the future of our dear fatherland.

Citizens, rally around the Provisional Government for the defence of its provisional authority in the name of order and the welfare of every people of our great fatherland. . . .

(e) The Origins of the Red Army

Source: Leon Trotsky, *Kak vooruzhalas revoliutsiia* (*na voennoi rabote*), tr. Bunyan and Fisher, op. cit., pp. 569–70.

In the beginning we could not resort to conscription. We had neither political nor other machinery for drafting the recently demobilized peasants. We called for volunteers and . . . although we got a number of self-sacrificing young workmen, the majority of those who enlisted were vagabonds of the worst kind. . . .

The political difficulties and the problem of organization were exceedingly great. The psychological break from the decay of the old army to the formation of the new led to constant internal frictions and conflicts. . . .

A real army cannot be run by elected committees and elected officers who may be dismissed at any moment by their subordinates. But the army did not even intend to fight. It was carrying on a social revolution within itself by overthrowing its bourgeois officers and forming . . . Soviets of Soldiers' Deputies. These [changes] were desirable . . . from the point of view of destroying the old army, but they did not create a new one. The tsarists regiments that survived the Kerensky régime broke up after November and then vanished entirely. . . . The Red Army was an institution built from the top on the principle of the dictatorship of the working class, with officers selected and controlled by the Soviet Government and the Communist Party . . . [But] the Socialist-Revolutionists of the Left wished to carry the pseudo-democratic principle to an absurdity. They demanded that each regiment should be allowed to decide for itself whether it would comply with the terms of the German armistice or would go on fighting. In this way the Socialist-Revolutionists of the Left attempted to stir up the army against its organizer, the Soviet Government.

The old officers who remained in our service were either idealists, who understood the meaning of the new epoch (they were, of course, an insignificant minority), or time-servers, men without initiative, without principles, and without even enough energy to join the Whites. A great many active counter-revolutionists . . . also remained with us.

We had to consider these tsarist officers for reasons of their professional training. . . . Without them we should have had to begin from the beginning, and it was not likely that our enemies would have given us the time needed to carry our self-education to the necessary level. We could not build up a centralized army . . . without making use of the . . . old officers; they were to come in, however, not as representatives of the old ruling class but as appointees of the new revolutionary class. It is true that many of them betrayed us and went over to the enemy . . . but it is equally true that the backbone of their class resistance was broken.

The institution of (military) commissars played a most important part in the formation of the commanding staff. The commander occupied himself with purely military matters and the commissar with political-educational work. The important thing, however, was that the commissar functioned as the direct representative of the Soviet Government in the army. A commissar was not in any way to interfere with nor to do anything to lower the authority of the commander but was to strive to bring about a state of affairs that would make it impossible for the commander to use his authority against the revolution. The working class gave its best sons to this office. Hundreds and thousands of them died performing the duties of commissar and many of them rose to the rank of commander.

34. The Communist State

(a) Collectivization

Victor Serge (1890–1947) was an anarchist in France, and in 1919 a member of the Comintern in Russia. He wrote and worked against the authoritarian aspects of Stalinism, was exiled, and died in Mexico City.

Source: Victor Serge, *Memoirs of a Revolutionary*, tr. Peter Sedgwick, pp. 246–8.

The real policy had been outlined by Molotov at the Fifteenth Party Congress: the development of collective agricultural cultivation (kolkhozes) or of State grain-factories (sovkhozes). A slow development was envisaged, spread over many years, since collective agriculture could only replace piecemeal cultivation stage by stage as the State supplied the farms with the equipment that was indispensable to mechanized cultivation. But, as it was, war had been declared on the peasantry through the requisitioning. If the State confiscates the grain, what is the use of sowing? In the following spring, statistics will show that the area under wheat has shrunk: a peasants' strike. There is only one way of forcing them: compulsory co-operatives, administered by the Communists. Will persuasion succeed? The independent farmer who has resisted the agitation, or rather coercion, turns out to be freer and better fed than his fellows. The Government draws the conclusion that collectivization must be total and abrupt. However, the folk of the soil are putting up a bitter defence. How can their resistance be broken? By expropriation and mass deportation of the rich peasants or kulaks and of any that may be classified as kulaks. This is what is called 'the liquidation of the kulaks as a class'.

Will it ever be known how terrible was the disorganization of agriculture that resulted? Rather than hand over their livestock to the kolkhoz, the peasants slaughter the beasts, sell the meat and make boots out of the leather. Through the destruction of its livestock the country passes from poverty to famine. Bread-cards in the cities, black market, a slump in the rouble and in real wages. Internal passports have to be issued, to keep the skilled manpower in the factories against its will. Since total collectivization is heading towards disaster, its completion is declared when it has reached 68 per cent, and even then too late, in March 1930, when famine and terror are at their height.

The women came to deliver the cattle confiscated by the kolkhoz, but made a rampart of their own bodies around the beasts: 'Go on, bandits shoot!' And why should these rebels not be shot at? In a Kuban market-town whose entire population was deported, the women undressed in their houses, thinking that no one would dare make them go out naked; they were driven out as they were to the cattle-trucks, beaten with rifle-butts. Cheboldayev of the Central Committee was in charge of the mass deportation in this region, never suspecting that, for his very enthusiasm, he would be shot in 1937. Terror reigned in the smallest hamlets. There were more than 300 centres of peasant insurrection going on simultaneously in Soviet Eurasia.

Trainloads of deported peasants left for the icy North, the forests, the steppes, the deserts. These were whole populations, denuded of everything; the old folk starved to death in mid-journey, new-born babies were buried on the banks of the roadside, and each wilderness had its crops of little crosses of boughs or white wood. Other populations, dragging all their mean possessions on wagons, rushed towards the frontiers of Poland, Rumania, and China and crossed them—by no means intact, to be sure—in spite of the machine-guns. And in a long message to the

Government, couched in a noble style, the population of Abkhazia pleaded for permission to emigrate to Turkey.

A Russian scholar, Prokopovich, made the following calculation from official Soviet statistics—at a time, be it noted, when the statisticians were being imprisoned and shot. Up to 1929 the number of peasants' households grew uninterruptedly:

1928: 24,500,000 households
1929: 25,800,000 households

When collectivization ended in 1936, there were no more than 20,600,000 households. In seven years over 5,000,000 families disappeared.

The transport system was worn down, and all plans for industrialization were turned inside-out to cope with the new demands. It was, to quote Boris Souvarine's expression, 'the anarchy of the plan'. Agricultural technicians and experts were brave in denouncing the blunders and excesses; they were arrested in thousands and made to appear in huge sabotage-trials so that responsibility might be unloaded on somebody. The rouble was in the process of disappearing; hoarders of silver coin were shot (1930). Crisis in the coal industry, Shakhty sabotage-trial, fifty-three technicians in court, executions. Naturally there is a meat shortage: execution of Professor Karatygin and his forty-seven co-defendants for sabotage of the meat supply —an execution without trial.

(b) Industrialization and Electrification

GOELRO, or State Commission for Electrification, was set up on Lenin's initiative, in 1920, with Krzhizhanovsky as President. He wrote this about their plan.

Source: Report to the 5th Congress of Soviets, quoted in M. Dobb, *Soviet Economic Development since 1917*, p. 335.

Our country was still in the midst of the calamity of war; we were still continuing to roll into the abyss of deepest economic disorder. And then, according to directives of the Party, there was created the first perspective economic plan. We proceeded to collect a handful of people, scientific and technical workers, and under the immediate guidance of Vladimir Ilyitch (Lenin), we tried to pick our way among the economic chaos surrounding us, tried to harness to the conquest of science and technique those active elements among the workers and peasants whose creative power we perceived and recognised in the midst of ruin and war. In this plan we daringly sketched an impression of our future, a design of that building which we can and must convert into reality. Very soon we were assailed with banter: people said that it was not a plan of electrification but of 'electric-fiction'; they said it was poetry, an imaginative creation, far from reality.

(c) Stalin's Speech to Industrial Managers, February 1931

This famous speech sums up Stalin's determination to industrialize Russia at all costs; it shows how powerful nationalism had become in the Communist state, and it might be taken as the dominant theme in Soviet agriculture, industry, foreign policy, and attitudes to the West.

Source: J. Stalin, 'Problems of Leninism' quoted in I. Deutscher, *Stalin*, p. 328.

. . . No, comrades. . . . the pace must not be slackened! On the contrary, we must quicken it as much as is within our powers and possibilities. This is dictated to us by our obligations to the workers and peasants of the U.S.S.R. This is dictated to us by our obligations to the working class of the whole world.

To slacken the pace would mean to lag behind; and those who lag behind are beaten. We do not want to be beaten. No, we don't want to. The history of old . . .

Russia . . . she was ceaselessly beaten for her backwardness. She was beaten by the Mongol Khans, she was beaten by Turkish Beys, she was beaten by Swedish feudal lords, she was beaten by Polish-Lithuanian Pans, she was beaten by Anglo-French capitalists, she was beaten by Japanese barons, she was beaten by all—for her backwardness. For military backwardness, for cultural backwardness, for political backwardness, for industrial backwardness, for agricultural backwardness. She was beaten because to beat her was profitable and went unpunished. You remember the words of the pre-revolutionary poet: 'Thou art poor and thou art plentiful, thou art mighty and thou art helpless, Mother Russia.'

. . . We are fifty or a hundred years behind the advanced countries. We must make good this lag in ten years. Either we do it or they crush us. . . .

Italy

35. Mazzini and Young Italy, 1832

The extract is from a paper in which Mazzini set out the new society's ideals.

Source: *Life and Writings of Joseph Mazzini*, I, 96 ff., in Robinson and Beard, pp. 115–17.

LIBERTY—EQUALITY—HUMANITY— INDEPENDENCE—UNITY

Young Italy is a brotherhood of Italians who believe in a law of progress and duty, and are convinced that Italy is destined to become one nation, convinced also that she possesses sufficient strength within herself to become one, and that the ill success of her former efforts is to be attributed not to the weakness, but to the misdirection of the revolutionary elements within her, that the secret force lies in constancy and unity of effort. They join this association with the firm intention of consecrating both thought and action to the great aim of reconstituting Italy as one independent sovereign nation of free men and equals. . . .

The aim of the association is revolution; but its labours will be essentially educational, both before and after the day of revolution; and it therefore declares the principles upon which the national education should be conducted, and from which alone Italy may hope for safety and regeneration. . . .

Young Italy is republican and unitarian,[11]—republican,

[11] That is, opposes a federal system.

because theoretically every nation is destined, by the law of God and humanity, to form a free and equal community of brothers; and the republican government is the only form of government that insures this future: because all true sovereignty resides essentially in the nation, the sole progressive and continuous interpreter of the supreme moral law; . . .

Our Italian tradition is essentially republican; our great memories are republican; the whole history of our national progress is republican; whereas the introduction of monarchy amongst us was coeval with our decay, and consummated our ruin by its constant servility to the foreigner and antagonism to the people as well as to the unity of the nation.

* * *

Young Italy is unitarian, because, without unity there is no true nation; because, without unity there is no real strength; and Italy, surrounded as she is by powerful, united, and jealous nations, has need of strength above all things; because federalism, by reducing her to the political impotence of Switzerland, would necessarily place her under the influence of one of the neighbouring nations; because federalism, by reviving the local rivalries now extinct, would throw Italy back upon the Middle Ages; . . . because federalism, by destroying the unity of the great Italian family, would strike at the root of the great mission Italy is destined to accomplish for humanity; because Europe is undergoing a progressive series of transformations, which are gradually and irresistibly guiding European society to form itself into vast and united masses; because the entire work of internal civilization in Italy will be seen, if rightly studied, to have been tending for ages towards unity.

The means by which Young Italy proposes to reach its

aim are education and insurrection, to be adopted simultaneously and made to harmonize with each other. Education must ever be directed to teach, by example, word, and pen, the necessity of insurrection. Insurrection, whenever it can be realized, must be so conducted as to render it a means of national education. Education, though of necessity secret in Italy, will be public outside of Italy. . . .

Insurrection, by means of guerrilla bands, is the true method of warfare for all nations desirous of emancipating themselves from a foreign yoke. This method of warfare supplies the want—inevitable at the commencement of the insurrection—of a regular army; it calls the greatest number of elements into the field, and yet may be sustained by the smallest number. It forms the military education of the people and consecrates every foot of the native soil by the memory of some warlike deed. Guerrilla warfare opens a field of activity for every local capacity, forces the enemy into an unaccustomed method of battle, avoids the evil consequences of a great defeat, secures the national war from the risk of treason, and has the advantage of not confining it within any defined and determinate basis of operations. It is invincible, indestructible. The regular army, recruited with all possible solicitude and organized with all possible care, will complete the work begun by the war of insurrection.

All the members of Young Italy will exert themselves to diffuse these principles of insurrection. The association will develop them more fully in its writings, and will explain from time to time the ideas and organization which should govern the period of insurrection.

36. Revolution, 1848-49

(a) The Situation in Venetia

The English Consul-General wrote the following dispatch on 18 January 1848.

Source: *British & Foreign State Papers*, XXXVII, 835 ff., in Robinson and Beard, pp. 96–99.

Though the Venetian provinces have hitherto been much more tranquil than the provinces of Lombardy, they appear now disposed to make common cause with the latter, and it is surprising to see the change that a short time has brought about.

When I left Venice, early in November last, everything was perfectly quiet, and although some little excitement had been produced by the speeches delivered by a few persons during the sitting of the Scientific Congress, society was upon its accustomed footing. Now, however, it is quite different; the Venetians have adopted the system of the Milanese, and there is hardly a Venetian house into which an Austrian is admitted. This determination has been come to very unwillingly by many, but they act under a system of intimidation that is carried on to a degree scarcely credible. Persons supposed to have a leaning towards the government are held up to public execration, and their names are written upon the walls as traitors to their country. . . .

Should a collision ensue between the troops and the people,—and a very slight thing may bring it on—the consequences, I fear, would be extremely serious.

(b) Milan's Appeal to Sardinia

In this document the provisional government of Milan appealed for aid to Charles Albert, King of Sardinia, 23 March 1848.

Source: op. cit., p. 959.

Sacred Majesty:

We have vanquished the enemy who occupied the city. He left the castle last night and marched towards Verona, but he is not yet far from the capital and is marking every step with slaughter and plunder. Our citizens have made heroic efforts, and with very few resources they have repulsed the pride of an enemy confident in his strength. . . .

Although the city is now free, the speedy and potent aid of your Majesty is none the less important. The provisional government therefore implores your Majesty to hasten to assist us by every means. Your Majesty will thus be a benefactor to the sacred cause of Italian independence and brotherhood, and will surely receive the applause and gratitude of this people. We would willingly add more, but our position as a provisional government does not allow us to anticipate the wishes of the nation, which are, without doubt, all directed towards the furtherance of the cause of Italian unity.

(c) The Roman Republic

The Convention of Rome proclaimed the Roman Republic, 9 February 1849 in this decree.

Source: *State Papers* (1854–55), pp. 353–4.

Art. I. The Papacy has forfeited in fact and of right the temporal government of the Roman State.

II. The Roman pontiff shall have all the guarantees necessary to secure his independence in the exercise of his spiritual power.

III. The form of the government of the Roman State shall be a pure democracy, and it shall take the glorious name of the Roman Republic.

IV. The Roman Republic shall maintain such relations

with the rest of Italy as our common nationality may require.

February 9th, 1949, 1 o'clock in the morning.

G. Galetti, President.

[It was followed by a proclamation:]

Long Live the Roman Republic!

Rome, February 8th [1849].

It is 1 o'clock, after midnight, and we issue at this moment from the hall where the convention has been assembled since 11 o'clock a.m. Who can describe the commotions which have agitated us? The great word has been pronounced.

Democracy has won the day. After a serious, animated, but free and conscientious discussion, at a quarter past 11 p.m., amidst the applause of the people assembled in crowds in the galleries, the Roman Republic was proclaimed, after the fall of the temporal power of the Pope had been declared. Out of more than 140 representatives of the people only some twenty were against the propositions that were passed.

In this manner religion has been purified. Italy has recovered Rome, and Rome has opened to itself a glorious future. The majority of the representatives agreeing in this great proclamation demonstrates fully that the desire of the people to be emancipated from a theocratic government could no longer be repressed.

*　　*　　*

(d) Sardinia's Constitutional Charter

Charles Albert gave to Sardinia a Constitutional Charter, of which the main outlines are made clear in this summary attached to it: it became the foundation of the government of United Italy.

Source: *Annual Register* of 1848, pp. 317–18.

We have much pleasure in declaring that, with the advice and approval of our ministers and the principal advisers of our crown, we have resolved and determined to adopt the following bases of a fundamental statute for the establishment in our States of a complete system of representative government.

ART. 1. The Catholic, apostolic, and Roman religion is the sole religion of the State. Other forms of public worship at present existing are tolerated in conformity with the law.

ART. 2. The person of the sovereign is sacred and inviolable. His ministers are responsible.

ART. 3. The executive power is vested in the king alone. He is the supreme head of the State. He commands all the forces, both naval and military; declares war, concludes treaties of peace, alliance, and commerce; nominates to all offices, and gives all the necessary orders for the execution of the laws, without, however, suspending them or dispensing with the observance thereof.

Art. 4. The king alone sanctions and promulgates the laws.

Art. 5. All justice emanates from the king, and is administered in his name. He may grant mercy and commute punishment.

ART. 6. The legislative power will be collectively exercised by the King and by two Chambers.

ART. 7. The first of these Chambers will be composed of members nominated by the King for life; the second shall be elective, on the basis of a census to be determined later.

ART. 8. The proposal of laws will appertain to the King and in each of the Chambers, but with the distinct understanding that all laws imposing taxes must originate in the elective Chamber.

ART. 9. The King convokes the two Chambers annually;

he prorogues their sessions, and may dissolve the elective Chamber; but in this case he will convoke a new assembly at the expiration of four months.

ART. 10. No tax may be imposed or levied unless approved by the Chambers and sanctioned by the King.

ART. 11. The press shall be free, but subject to laws for its control.

ART. 12. Individual liberty will be guaranteed.

37. The Risorgimento, 1858–70

(a) French Aid

Napoleon III's explanation of why he was about to intervene in the Italian Question, May 1859.

Source: *Le Moniteur universel*, 4 May 1859, in Robinson and Beard, pp. 122–3.

Frenchmen, Austria in ordering her army to invade the territory of the King of Sardinia, our ally, has declared war upon us. She has thus violated treaties and justice and threatens our frontiers. All the great powers have protested against this aggression.

Piedmont having accepted conditions which should have maintained peace, one cannot but inquire what can be the reason for this sudden invasion on Austria's part. It is because Austria has brought matters to such a pass that either she must dominate as far as the Cottian Alps, or Italy must be freed to the Adriatic; for every corner of territory which remains independent in that whole region is a menace to her authority.

Hitherto moderation has been the rule of my conduct; now an aggressive policy becomes my duty. Let France arm herself and say to Europe with determination: 'We do not wish for conquest, but we are resolved to maintain without flinching our national and traditional policy; we observe treaties on condition that they shall not be violated to our disadvantage; we respect the territory and the rights of neutral powers, but openly avow our sympathy for a people whose history is bound up with ours, and who groan under foreign oppression.'

France has shown her hatred of anarchy; she has been pleased to give me an authority strong enough to render powerless the abettors of disorder and the incorrigible members of former factions who have not hesitated to form alliances with our enemies; but she has not, on that account, abandoned her function as a civilizing power. Her natural allies have always been those who desire the improvement of humanity, and when she draws her sword it is not in order to domineer, but to liberate.

The purpose of this war is, then, to restore Italy to herself, not simply to change her master; and we shall have upon our frontiers a friendly people who will owe their independence to us. We are not going into Italy to foment disorder, nor to disturb the authority of the Holy Father, whom we have replaced upon his throne, but to protect him against that foreign oppression which weighs upon the whole peninsula, and to participate in establishing order there which shall satisfy all legitimate interests. We are, in short, about to enter that classic land rendered illustrious by so many victories. We shall find there traces of our forefathers, of whom God grant we may prove ourselves worthy. . . .

Napoleon

Palace of the Tuileries, 3 May 1859.

(b) The Duchies

The Tuscans expelled their Grand Duke and a provisional government issued this document on 29 September 1859.

Source: *British and Foreign State Papers* (1858–59), Robinson and Beard, p. 123.

The Assembly of your lawful representatives has declared it to be the firm desire of Tuscany to form a part of a strong constitutional kingdom under the sceptre of King Victor Emmanuel of the House of Savoy. The Assemblies of Modena, Parma, and the Romagna have unanimously issued similar declarations. The king-elect has accepted the free act of subjection on the part of the people of Tuscany, Modena, Parma, and the Romagna, and has declared that the first act of his sovereignty should be formally to sanction the rights which had been conferred on him by those peoples.

* * *

The war undertaken by Napoleon and Victor Emmanuel was a solemn recognition of that right, since it was undertaken to liberate Italy from Austrian dominion and to constitute Italian nationality. All Italians were called on to profit by the great occasion, and the people of central Italy flew to arms. The Tuscans had the double honour of fighting under the glorious Italian banner and under the invincible eagles of the French empire. . . .

But if the present government is to govern for His Majesty until the king-elect assumes personal rule over the Tuscans, it should also glory in and strengthen itself under his august name. In this way the new settlement of the Italian nation will proceed with security, every obstacle will gradually disappear, and Europe will be indebted for its tranquillity and its true equilibrium to the union and firmness of the Italians.

Tuscans! Your government proclaims that it will for the future exercise its power in the name of His Majesty Victor Emmanuel of Savoy, the king-elect.

Given at Florence, the 29th September, 1859.

(c) **An Italian Parliament**

Victor Emmanuel's address to a Parliament representative of the freed provinces, on 2 April 1860 at Turin.

Source: *Annuaire historique universel* for 1860, Appendix, pp. 148 ff. in Robinson and Beard, pp. 125–6.

The last time that I opened this parliament, in the midst of the travails of Italy and dangers to the State, faith in divine justice encouraged me to prophesy a happy issue for us. In a very short space of time an invasion has been repelled; Lombardy has been freed, thanks to the glorious exploits of our heroes, and central Italy has been delivered, thanks to the remarkable courage of its inhabitants; and today the representatives of right and of the hopes of the nation are assembled about me.

We owe many benefits to a magnanimous ally, to the bravery of his soldiers as well as of ours, to the self-abnegation of the volunteers, and to the harmony of the various peoples; and we render thanks to God, for without superhuman aid these enterprises, memorable not only for our own generation but for ages to come, could not have been achieved.

Out of gratitude to France for the services she has rendered to Italy, and in order to consolidate the union of the two nations, which have a community of origin, of principles, and of destiny, some sacrifice was necessary; I have made that one which costs most to my own heart. Subject to the vote of the people and the approbation of the parliament, . . . I have agreed to a treaty providing for the reunion of Savoy and of the district of Nice to France.

We still have many difficulties to overcome, but sustained by public opinion and by the love of the people, I will not permit any right or liberty to be infringed or diminished.

Although I am as consistent in my respect towards the

supreme head of our religion as the Catholic rulers, my ancestors, have always shown themselves, nevertheless, should the ecclesiastical authority resort to spiritual arms in support of its temporal interests, I will, relying upon a pure conscience and the traditions of my forefathers, find strength to maintain civil liberty and my authority, for the exercise of which I owe an account only to God and to my people. . . .

(d) Garibaldi's Invasion of Sicily and Naples, May 1860

Garibaldi's own account (condensed here) was written, from memory, in 1872 on Caprera.

Source: *Autobiography of Giuseppe Garibaldi*, tr. A. Werner, 1889, Vol. II, pp. 144-61, 204-6, 215-17.

Sicily: Austria is powerful, her armies are numerous; several formidable neighbours are opposed, on account of petty dynastic aims, to the resurrection of Italy. The Bourbon has a hundred thousand soldiers. Yet what matter? the heart of twenty-five millions throbs and trembles with the love of their country! Sicily, coming forward as champion and representative of these millions, impatient of servitude, has thrown down the gauntlet to tyranny, and defies it everywhere, combating it alike within convent walls and on the peaks of her ever-active volcanoes. But her heroes are few, while the ranks of the tyrant are numerous; and the patriots are scattered, driven from the capital, and forced to take to the mountains. But are not the mountains the refuge, the sanctuary, of the liberty of nations? The Americans, the Swiss, the Greeks, held the mountains when overpowered by the ordered cohorts of their oppressors. 'Liberty never escapes those who truly desire to win her.' Well has this been proved true by those resolute islanders, who, driven from the cities, kept up the sacred fire in the mountains. Weariness, hardships, sacrifices—what do they matter, when men are fighting for the sacred cause of their country, of humanity?

To board the two steamers at anchor in the harbour at Genoa, just under the 'Darsena', to overpower the crew and force them to assist us, then to get up steam and take the 'Lombardo' in tow of the 'Piemonte', and all this by moonlight—these are actions easier to describe than to perform, and needing great coolness, skill, and good fortune to execute them successfully. The two Sicilians, Orlando and Campo, who formed part of the expedition, and were both engineers, were of the greatest use to us on this occasion.

By dawn all were on board. The joy of danger and adventure, and the consciousness of serving their country's sacred cause, were stamped on the countenances of the Thousand.

They were glorious, my young veterans of Italian liberty; and I, proud of their faith in me, felt capable of attempting anything.

During the voyage the whole of the men had been divided into eight companies, the most distinguished officers of the expedition being placed at the head of each. Sirtori was appointed chief of staff; Acerbi, quartermaster; and Türr, staff-officer. The arms had been distributed, as also the few clothes we had been able to get together before our departure.

Our first idea was to land at Sciacca, but as the day was advanced, and we were afraid of meeting the enemy's cruisers, we resolved to put into the nearest port, that of Marsala (May 11, 1860).

As we approached the western coast of Sicily, we began to discover sailing-vessels and steamers. On the roadstead of Marsala two men-of-war were anchored, which turned out to be English. Having decided on landing at Marsala, we approached that port, and reached it about noon. On entering the harbour, we found it full of merchant vessels of different nations.

Fortune had indeed favoured us, and so guided our expedition that we could not have arrived at a more propitious moment.

The Bourbon cruisers had left the harbour of Marsala that morning, sailing eastward, while we were arriving from the west; indeed, they were still in sight towards Cape San Marco, as we entered—so that, by the time they came within cannon-shot, we had already landed all the men out of the 'Piemonte', and were beginning to disembark those on board the 'Lombardo'.

The presence of the two English men-of-war in some degree influenced the determination of the Bourbon commanders, who were naturally impatient to open fire on us, and this circumstance gave us time to get our whole force on shore. The noble English flag once more helped to prevent bloodshed, and I, the Benjamin of these lords of the ocean, was for the hundredth time protected by them.

The assertion, however, made by our enemies, that the English had directly favoured and assisted our landing at Marsala, was inaccurate.

The population of Marsala, thunderstruck at this unexpected event, received us pretty well, all things considered. The common people, indeed, were delighted; the magnates welcomed us under protest. I thought all this very natural. Those who are accustomed to calculate everything at so much per cent., are not likely to be reassured by the sight of a few desperadoes, who wish to ameliorate a corrupt society by eradicating from it the cancer of privilege and falsehood—especially when these desperadoes, few in number as they are, and with neither three-hundred-pounders nor ironclads, fling themselves against a power believed to be gigantic, like that of the Bourbon.

The Mainland. Having reached the strait, it became necessary to cross it. To have reinstated Sicily in the great Italian family was certainly a glorious achievement. But what then? Were we, in compliance with diplomacy, to leave our country incomplete and maimed? What of the two Calabrias, and Naples, awaiting us with open arms? And the rest of Italy still enslaved by the foreigner and the priest? We were clearly bound to pass the strait, despite the utmost vigilance of the Bourbons and their adherents. The splendid 'Torino' already had a large number of the thousand on board, and was in excellent condition. The 'Franklin', on the other hand, seemed to be sinking; she was nearly full of water, and the engineer declared that she could not possibly make the voyage in that state. Bixio was greatly annoyed by this, and was preparing to start with only the 'Torino.' However, being myself on board the 'Franklin', I ordered nearly all the officers on board to jump into the sea, dive, and try whether they could find the leak; while at the same time I sent on shore for a quantity of farmyard manure, in order to make what is called purina.[12] In this way we contrived to stop the leak to some extent; the engineer was pacified; and, it being known that I was going to cross by the 'Franklin' myself, the rest of the men began to come on board, so that by 10 p.m. we were under way for the Calabrian coast, which we reached in safety.

Naples. Our entry into the great capital sounds more imposing than it was in reality. Accompanied by a small staff, I passed through the midst of the Bourbon troops still in occupation, who presented arms far more obsequiously than they did at that time to their own generals.

[12] A kind of plaster, made by mixing chopped straw with the ingredient above mentioned, lumps of which are thrust under the ship, on the end of a pole, in the direction of the supposed leak. The water, rushing into the opening, naturally carries with it some of the straw, etc., and thus the leak is stopped, at any rate partially.

September 7th, 1860!—which of the sons of Parthenope will not remember that glorious day? On September 7th fell the abhorred dynasty which a great English statesman had called 'The curse of God', and on its ruins rose the sovereignty of the people, which, by some unhappy fatality, never lasts long.

On September 7th, a son of the people, accompanied by a few of his friends, who acted as his staff [13] entered the splendid capital of the fiery courser, [14] acclaimed and supported by its 500,000 inhabitants, whose fervid and irresistible will, paralysing an entire army, urged them to the demolition of a tyranny, and the vindication of their sacred rights. That shock might well have moved the whole of Italy, impelling it forward on the path of duty; that roar would suffice to tame the insolent and insatiable rulers, and overthrow them in the dust.

Though the Bourbon army was still in possession of the forts and the principal points of the city, whence they could easily have destroyed it, yet the applause and the impressive conduct of this great populace sufficed to ensure their harmlessness on September 7th, 1860.

I entered Naples with the whole of the southern army as yet a long way off in the direction of the Straits of Messina, the King of Naples having, on the previous day, quitted his palace to retire to Capua.

The royal nest, still warm, was occupied by the emancipators of the people, and the rich carpets of the royal palace were trodden by the heavy boots of the plebeian.

At Naples, as in all places we had passed through since crossing the strait, the populace were sublime in their enthusiastic patriotism, and the resolute tone assumed by them certainly had no small share in the brilliant results obtained.

[13] Missori, Nullo, Basso, Mario, Stagnetti, Canzio.
[14] The emblem of Naples.

Another circumstance very favourable to the national cause was the tacit consent of the Bourbon navy, which, had it been entirely hostile, could have greatly retarded our progress towards the capital. In fact, our steamers transported the divisions of the southern army along the whole Neapolitan coast without let or hindrance, which could not have been done in the face of any decided opposition on the part of the navy.

(e) The Taking of Rome, 20 September 1870

The British Ambassador's description.

Source: *British & Foreign State Papers*, LXII, 293 ff.

Florence, September 22nd, 1870.

All efforts at a pacific arrangement with the commander of the papal troops having failed, orders were sent to General Cadorna on the 19th instant to take possession of Rome by force; and accordingly, at 5 o'clock on the morning of the 20th instant, a cannonade was opened, two breaches were effected at half past 8, and at 10 o'clock the Italian troops entered the city between the Porta Pia and Porta Salara. The white flag was then hoisted by command of the Pope, hostilities ceased, and a capitulation was signed between General Kanzler, commander of the papal troops, and General Cadorna. There was no fighting in the streets. According to the terms of the capitulation, the papal forces had to lay down their arms. They are, or will be, sent to Civita Vecchia,—the natives to form a depot without arms, while the foreigners having no means to defray their expenses will be sent back to their own countries.

On the special demand of the Pope, transmitted through General Kanzler, General Cadorna has furnished two battalions for the purpose of maintaining order in the Leonine City. Castel St. Angelo was occupied for strategical reasons after the assault. The loss on the Italian side amounts to somewhat over one hundred in killed and wounded. A proof that the Pope ordered the defence, and that it was not, as erroneously asserted, the military element which was master of the situation and imposed its will on His Holiness, is that, as stated above, it was on the Pope's order that the firing ceased from the town, and that the garrison surrendered. . . .

I am informed that, since the entry of the troops, some of the foreign representatives in Rome have expressed to the Italian general their satisfaction at the conduct and bearing of the soldiers, as well as with the measures which have been taken for the preservation of order. The reception of the Italian army is described as having been enthusiastic. . . .

*   *   *

The news of the entry into Rome has been received throughout Italy with the utmost enthusiasm. In every town the streets have been hung with flags; there have been processions, bands of music, shoutings, illuminations, and, not the least remarkable of these demonstrations, considering their occasion, the bells of all the cathedrals and churches have been ringing out merry peals in honour of the deathblow inflicted upon the temporal power of the Holy Father.

The cry now is to transfer the capitol to Rome at once; and the 15th of October is spoken of by the press as the day when the Chamber is to meet to vote upon this subject. I doubt, however, if any decision in this sense has been taken by the government. Many things have to be arranged before the Chamber can be consulted on this subject; and, amongst them, communications with the Catholic powers would appear to be a necessary preliminary step.

38. The Economic Problems of Italy, 1906

The general nature of these problems is clear from this analysis published in 1906.

Source: *Journal des Economistes* (Paris, 1906), IX, 321 ff., in Robinson and Beard, pp. 138–41.

The official Bulletin on Emigration establishes the fact that during the year 1904 the number of emigrants was about 506,731. In 1903 it was 507,976; in 1902, 531,509; in 1901, 533,245; in 1900, 352,782. This exodus does not represent a total loss of population, because a considerable number of emigrants do not leave the country for good; a part of them—more than half—return. . . .

*   *   *

Nevertheless, in spite of this astounding rate of emigration, the increase in population has not only been constant since 1871, but has surpassed for some years the average annual increase of the other states of continental Europe which are the most prolific. The density of the population in Italy at present is about 115 inhabitants to the square kilometer, whilst it was but 99·28 in 1881. In France the density is about 73; in Germany, 104, in Austria, 87. To maintain this enormous and constantly increasing population, it would be necessary for the wealth of the country to increase in the same proportion and at the same rate. But this does not happen. The wealth of Italy does not keep pace with the increase of the population; and the nourishing earth, becoming powerless, sends forth her people to the four corners of the world.

According to statistics, the following is, approximately, the wealth per inhabitant in 1900 in different European countries:

England	.	.	.	6600 francs
France	.	.	.	5560 ,,
Germany	.	.	.	2840 ,,
Austria-Hungary	.		.	1960 ,,
Italy	.	.	.	1600 ,,

The total wealth of Italy, valued in francs at forty-six thousand millions in 1880, rose to fifty-two thousand millions in 1900; but this increase loses all importance if it is placed beside the increase in population, which was about four million inhabitants during the same period,— a large increase in spite of the already considerable exodus of emigrants.

No one will question the economic advance of Italy, I least of all. However, I am obliged to state that the supply of workmen in this country still exceeds the limit of the demand, that is to say, the power of absorption of available capital. This fact is the more evident since the agricultural development is not far behind the progress of industrial capitalism. In the north where industry is implanted in the midst of the fields, the question has been settled; the peasants go elsewhere to supplement their wages, and then return. But in the south the problem assumes a gravity quite different, for the lack of capital has prevented, up to the present time, a rational transformation, and on a sufficiently vast scale, of the methods of agricultural ex-ploitation.

To the south of Tuscany there commences a new world, the southlands of Italy, under conditions of sadness and misery. The Roman Campagna with the Pontine Marshes and the Maremmes, which unite them geographically, constitute the first evidence,—how eloquent, alas!—of the profound differences which mark the two portions of Italy. In one there is a feverish activity, a prosperity that time and labour will undoubtedly assure; in the other there is veritable desolation. A first characteristic of the south-lands from the point of view of agriculture is the immense extent of marshy land or land imperfectly cultivated. The great landed property dominates there; and, except in Apulia, is almost everywhere devoid of the necessary farming equipment. The untilled lands in Italy extend over a surface of 3,774,000 hectares. They are divided into 2,500,000 hectares of dry land, and 1,274,000 hectares of swampy land, and nine tenths of this waste area belongs to southern Italy, where untilled lands cover one fifth of the territory.

In spite of this, or rather because of these extremely distressing conditions in the south, taxation, oppressive in the north, literally exhausts agriculture in the south. The Italian land tax is, on the average, about 6·48 francs per hectare. It is about 3·41 francs in the Netherlands; 3·17 in France; 1·51 in Austria; 1·39 in Prussia; and 0·89 in England. If, on the other hand, one considers, instead of the tax on land, the tax on incomes, one finds that it rises to 11 per cent in France; in Prussia to 15 per cent; in Belgium to 18 per cent; in England to 22 per cent; in Italy to 24 per cent. . . .

39. Mussolini's Fascist State, 1922-39

(a) The March on Rome, 27 October 1922

Source: *The Times*, Monday, 30 October 1922 (condensed).

TRIUMPH OF THE FASCISTS. BOLDLY PLANNED COUP. REVOLUTION WITHOUT BLOODSHED.

(From our special correspondent.)

Chiasso—October 29th.

The first rumours that the Fascisti had begun their insurrection operations spread about midnight on Friday.

Everywhere they mobilised and requested the local prefects to transfer their powers to Fascisti. The railway stations, post and telegraph offices and other public buildings were occupied, particularly in the towns in Central Italy so that communications with Rome could be cut, and the capital thus isolated. From many centres in Tuscany parties of Fascisti immediately left for Rome, and it is rumoured that several thousand of them were within a short distance of the gates of the capital on Saturday.

So far as the incomplete information goes, it appears that there were practically no conflicts and that the revolutionary movement was carried out without bloodshed. . . . Almost everywhere, it seems, the officers of the Army, whose sympathy with the Fascisti movement is well known, have treated the Fascisti with friendliness and avoided the use of force, which explains the success of the coup. The text of Fascisti proclamation is as follows:—

'Fascists! Italians! The hour of decisive battle has struck. Four years ago this day the National Army launched a supreme offensive that led to victory. Today, the Army of Blackshirts seizes again the mutilated victory and, pointing desperately towards Rome, carries it back to the glories of the Capitol. The martial law of Fascism goes into full effect. Following upon an order of the Duce, military, political and administrative powers of the Executive of the Party are assumed by a secret Quadrumvirate [15] of action with dictatorial mandate.

The Army, the supreme safeguard of the nation must not participate in the struggle. The Fascists renew again their highest admiration for the Army of Vittoria Veneto. Neither do the Fascists march against the police and guards, but against the political class of feeble, weak-

[15] The Quadrumvirate: Michele Bianchi, Secretary General of the Fascist party; General De Bono, a significant indication of the Army's sympathies; De Vecchi, landowner and lawyer; Italo Balbo, ex-Army officer.

minded men who, in four long years, have not been able to give a true Government to our nation.

The bourgeoisie should know that the Fascists want to impose a unique discipline on the nation, and help all forces destined to increase the economic expansion and welfare of the nation. The labourers and workmen have nothing to fear from Fascist power. Their just rights will be loyally defended. We shall be generous with unarmed adversaries and inexorable with others.

The Fascists unsheath their sword in order to cut the too numerous Gordian knots which bind and vitiate Italian life. God, and the spirit of our 500,000 Dead are witnesses that only one impulse makes us act, only one will unites us, only one passion inflames us: that is to contribute to the salvation and greatness of the country. . . . Fascists of all Italy! We must and shall win! Long live Italy! Long live Fascism!'

The intervention of the King, who wished to avoid serious bloodshed and civil war, rendered any resistance futile, and marked the capitulation of the authorities of the State to the insurgents.

There were great demonstrations of loyalty to the King in Rome. The Pope has sent a circular letter to the Bishops, deploring the gravity of the situation, and inviting them to make efforts towards pacification.

Signor Mussolini remained the whole day at the office of the Popolo d'Italia, which is the headquarters of the movement, communicating by telephone with his lieutenants in Rome and elsewhere.

He will not leave Milan until he is invited by the King to form a cabinet. Besides the Premiership, he intends to reserve to himself the portfolios of Home and Foreign Affairs, distributing all the others to Fascisti, except a few destined for Nationalists and Populists.

(b) The Conquest of Abyssinia

Two extracts are illuminating examples of Mussolini's oratory, and of the appeal of Fascism; the third represents much opinion in the democracies.

This speech, at 6.30 p.m., 2 October 1935, was preceded by the congregating of the people in the main squares of all villages and towns. In Rome, Mussolini spoke in the Piazza Venezia.

Source: *Giornale d'Italia*, translated in *Keesing's Contemporary Archives*, 1935, pp. 1814, 2095.

A solemn hour is about to break in the history of our country. Twenty million Italians are at this moment gathered in the squares of all Italy. There are twenty million, but one heart, one will, one desire. This manifestation means that the identity between Italy and Fascism is perfect, absolute, and unalterable.

For many months the wheel of fate turns under the impulse of our calm determination and moves towards this goal. In the last few hours the rhythm has grown swifter; it cannot be stopped. It is not only an army which marches towards its objective. Forty-four million Italians march with this army, all united and alert. Let others try to commit the blackest injustice, taking away Italy's place in the sun. When, in 1915, Italy united her fate with the Allies, how many cries and how many promises? To fight the common victory Italy brought her supreme contribution of 670,000 dead, 480,000 disabled and more than a million wounded. When we went to the Table of that odious peace they gave us only the crumbs of the Colonial booty.

[Same place: May 5th 1936.]

Blackshirts of the revolution, men and women of all Italy, Italians and friends of Italy beyond the mountains and beyond the seas, listen!

Marshal Badoglio telegraphs: 'Today, May 5th, at

4 p.m. at the head of the victorious troops, I have entered Addis Ababa.'

During the thirty centuries of her history, Italy has lived many memorable hours, but this of today is certainly one of the most solemn. I announce to the Italian people and to the world, that peace is re-established. But it is strictly necessary that I should add that it is our peace, which is expressed in this simple, irrevocable, definitive proposition: Abyssinia is Italian—Italian in fact because occupied by our victorious armies, Italian by right because with the sword of Rome it is civilisation which triumphs over barbarism, justice which triumphs over cruel arbitrariness. . . .

We are ready to defend our brilliant victory with the same intrepid and inexorable decision with which we have gained it. We feel that in this way we are interpreting the will of the combatants in Africa, of those who are dead, who have gloriously fallen in battle and whose memory will be treasured for generations and generations in the heart of the whole Italian people.

. . . Blackshirts of the Revolution, men and women of all Italy, a stage of the journey has been reached. Let us continue the march in peace for the tasks which await us tomorrow and which we will face with our courage, with our faith, and with our will. Evviva l'Italia! May this cry reach the troops, who are perhaps awaiting it on African soil. And to this cry I add: Evviva l'esercito, Evviva il Re!

(c) Foreign Comment on the Consequences of the Abyssinian Crisis

Winston Churchill, then out of office, summarised the immense international consequences of the Abyssinian crisis.

Source: W. S. Churchill, *The Second World War*, I, 149–50.

In the fearful struggle against rearming Nazi Germany which I could feel approaching with inexorable strides, I was most reluctant to see Italy estranged, and even driven into the opposite camp. There was no doubt that the attack by one member of the League of Nations upon another at this juncture, if not resented, would be finally destructive of the League as a factor for welding together the forces which could alone control the might of resurgent Germany and the awful Hitler menace. More could perhaps be got out of the vindicated majesty of the League than Italy could ever give, withhold, or transfer. If therefore the League were prepared to use the united strength of all its members to curb Mussolini's policy, it was our bounden duty to take our share and play a faithful part. There seemed in all the circumstances no obligation upon Britain to take the lead herself. She had a duty to take account of her own weakness caused by the loss of air parity, and even more of the military position of France, in the face of German rearmament. One thing was clear and certain. Half-measures were useless for the League, and pernicious to Britain if she assumed its leadership. If we thought it right and necessary for the law and welfare of Europe to quarrel mortally with Mussolini's Italy, we must also strike him down. The fall of the lesser Dictator might combine and bring into action all the forces, and they were still overwhelming—which would enable us to restrain the greater Dictator, and thus prevent a second German war. . . .

Ever since the Stresa Conference Mussolini's preparations for the conquest of Abyssinia had been apparent. It was evident that British opinion would be hostile to such an act of Italian aggression. Those of us who saw in Hitler's Germany a danger not only to peace but to survival dreaded this movement of a first-class Power, as Italy was then rated, from our side to the other. I remember a dinner at which Sir Robert Vansittart and Mr. Duff Cooper, then only an Under-Secretary, were present, at which this adverse change in the balance of Europe was clearly foreseen. The project was mooted of some of us going out to see Mussolini in order to explain to him the inevitable effects which would be produced in Great Britain. Nothing came of this; nor would it have been of any good. Mussolini, like Hitler, regarded Britannia as a frightened, flabby old woman, who at the worst would only bluster, and was anyhow incapable of making war. Lord Lloyd, who was on friendly terms with him, noted how he had been struck by the Joad resolution of the Oxford undergraduates in 1933 refusing to 'fight for King and Country'.

The Lesser States

40. Spain:

(a) The Revolt of the South American Colonies, and the Monroe Doctrine, 1823

The successful revolt of the Spanish colonies against the mother country and the possibility that the Congress powers might intervene on her behalf, led the President of the U.S.A., Monroe, to make this declaration in his message to Congress, 2 December 1823.

Source: *Annual Register*, 1823, p. 184.

It was stated at the commencement of the last session that a great effort was then making in Spain and Portugal to improve the condition of the people of those countries, and that it appeared to be conducted with extraordinary moderation. It need scarcely be remarked that the result has been so far very different from what was then anticipated. Of events in that quarter of the globe, with which we have so much intercourse and from which we derive our origin, we have always been anxious and interested spectators. The citizens of the United States cherish sentiments the most friendly in favour of the liberty and happiness of their fellow-men on that side of the Atlantic. In the wars of the European powers, in matters relating to themselves, we have never taken any part, nor does it comport with our policy so to do. It is only when our rights are invaded or seriously menaced that we resent injuries or make preparations for our defence.

With the movements in this hemisphere we are of necessity more immediately connected, and by causes which must be obvious to all enlightened and impartial observers.

The political system of the allied powers is essentially different in this respect from that of America. This difference proceeds from that which exists in their respective governments; and to the defence of our own which has been achieved by the loss of so much blood and treasure, and matured by the wisdom of their most enlightened citizens and under which we have enjoyed unexampled felicity, this whole nation is devoted. We owe it, therefore, to candour and to the amicable relations existing between the United States and those powers, to declare that we should consider any attempt on their part to extend their system to any portion of this hemisphere as dangerous to our peace and safety.

With the existing colonies or dependencies of any European power we have not interfered, and shall not interfere. But with the governments who have declared their independence and maintained it, and whose independence we have, on great consideration and on just principles, acknowledged, we could not view any interposition for the purpose of oppressing them, or controlling in any other manner their destiny, by any European power in any other light than as the manifestation of an unfriendly disposition towards the United States. . . .

(b) The Civil War, 1936–39

Guernica became a horrific symbol of this war. Great efforts were made by Franco's side and the Germans to put the blame on the Republicans, but this account seems substantially true.

Source: *The Times*, 28 April 1937.

THE TRAGEDY OF GUERNICA.
TOWN DESTROYED IN AIR ATTACK.
EYE WITNESSES'S ACCOUNT.

From Our Special Correspondent.

Bilbao April 27th.

Guernica, the most ancient town of the Basques, and the centre of their cultural tradition, was completely destroyed yesterday afternoon by insurgent air raiders.

The whole of Guernica was soon in flames except the historic Casa de Juntas with its rich archives of the Basque race, where the ancient Basque Parliament used to sit. The famous oak of Guernica, the dried old stump of 600 years and the new young shoots of this century was also untouched. Here the kings of Spain used to take the oath to respect the democratic rights of Vizcaya, and in return received a promise of allegiance as suzerains with the democratic title of Señor, not Rey Vizcaya.

At 2 a.m. today, when I visited the town, the whole of it was a horrible sight, flaming from end to end. Many of the civilian survivors took the long trek from Guernica to Bilbao in antique solid wheeled Basque farm carts drawn by oxen. Carts piled high with such household possessions as could be saved from the conflagration clogged the roads all night.

Guernica was not a military objective. A factory producing war material lay outside the town and was untouched. Of two barracks on the outskirts containing small forces, one was untouched and in the other only one man was killed. The town lay far behind the lines. The object was seemingly the demoralization of the civil population and the destruction of the cradle of the Basque race.

Monday was the customary market day in Guernica for the country round. At 4.30 p.m., when the market was full and peasants were still coming in, the church bell rang the alarm and the population sought refuge in cellars and dugouts. The people are said to have shown good spirit. A Catholic priest took charge and perfect order was maintained.

Five minutes later a single German bomber appeared, circled over the town at a low altitude, and then dropped six heavy bombs, apparently aiming for the station. The bombs with a shower of grenades fell on a former institute and on houses and streets surrounding it. In another five minutes came a second bomber which threw the same number of bombs into the middle of the town. About a quarter of an hour later, three Junkers arrived, and thenceforth the bombing grew in intensity and was continuous, ceasing only with dusk at 7.45. The whole town of 7,000 inhabitants plus 3,000 refugees was slowly and systematically pounded to pieces. Over a radius of five miles a detail of the raiders' technique was to bomb separate 'caserios' or farmhouses. In the night these burned like little candles in the hills.

Fighting machines swooped low to machine-gun those who ran in panic from dugouts. Many were killed as they ran. A large herd of sheep being brought in to market was also wiped out.

The only counter measures the Basques could employ were those provided by the heroism of the Basque clergy. These blessed and prayed for the kneeling crowds— Socialists, Anarchists and Communists, as well as the declared faithful—in the crumbling dugouts.

41. Belgium

(a) The Revolt against the Dutch, 1830

The Belgians proclaimed themselves independent of Holland on 5 October 1830, and the senior member of the Provisional government, Potter, addressed this message to the National Congress.

Source: *British and Foreign State Papers*, XVII, pp. 1238–41, in Butterfield, pp. 117–18.

Gentlemen:

In the name of the Belgian people, the Provisional Government opens the Assembly of the Representatives of the Nation.

These Representatives the Nation has entrusted with the august work of building on the wide and solid foundations of liberty the fabric of the new social order, which shall be the starting-point and the security for enduring happiness for Belgium.

You are aware, Gentlemen, that at the time of our union with Holland, a Fundamental Law was presented to the Notables, designed by the authorities not to be examined, discussed, modified and finally accepted, so as to be the condition of a Pact between the People and the Head of the State, but merely to be accepted blindly or rejected in its entirety. It was rejected, as might have been foretold, by the good sense and loyalty of Belgium. But by an unparalleled trick it was declared accepted; and a Constitution imposed by Holland was forced upon our Country.

Even so, if this Fundamental Law had been honestly carried out in all its provisions, perhaps in the course of time and with the help of that progress which we were making in the career of constitutional opposition as a result of the arbitrary conduct of ministers, it might have become the hope of Belgian liberty.

On the contrary: consciences violated, education fettered; the press doomed to be either the tool of authority or reduced to silence; the arbitrary substitution of a Despotic régime in the place of the legal system established by the social Pact; the right of petition disregarded; the confusion of the [governmental] powers and their combination in one person; the despotic establishment of a privileged language; the irremovability of Judges who were reduced to being the agents of power; the complete absence of the security which comes from publicity and trial by jury; an enormous debt and expenditure, the only dowry which Holland brought at the time of our deplorable union; taxes which are crushing both by their size and still more by their thoroughly anti-democratic distribution, completely to the disadvantage of the poorer classes; Laws always voted by the Dutchmen and with only the interests of Holland in view—always against the interests of Belgium, which was so unfairly represented in the old States-General; the seat of all the great constituted assemblies and all the important offices established in Holland, too; the scandalous squandering of money specially intended to favour industry; and finally, the most revolting partiality in the distribution of civil and military offices, by a Government in whose eyes the name of Belgian was a term of contempt; in sum, the whole of Belgium treated as a conquered Province or a Colony; everything, Gentlemen, made revolution necessary, and made it inevitable, and hastened its occurrence.

Grievances so just and genuine were bound also to ensure its success.

We have risen against despotism in order to win back our rights; we were treated as Rebels by our tyrants. Our towns were burned, the most barbarous crimes were committed even against old men and women, the laws of humanity and the laws of war were trampled underfoot, and these things testify to the ferocity of our Foes, and at the same time sanctify the victory of the People which has cleared them out of the land.

The fruit of this victory was Independence. The People has announced this through us. As the interpreter of its desires, the Provisional Government has called you, Gentlemen, the elected representatives of the Belgian Nation, to constitute this Independence and consolidate it for ever.

(b) The Guarantee of Belgian Neutrality, 1839

Source: E. Herslet, *The Map of Europe by Treaty* (1875–91), II, No. 183, in Mowat, pp. 37–38.

TREATY BETWEEN GREAT BRITAIN, AUSTRIA, FRANCE, PRUSSIA, AND RUSSIA, ON THE ONE PART, AND THE NETHERLANDS ON THE OTHER.

(London) April 19, 1839.

Article I. His Majesty the King of the Netherlands, Grand Duke of Luxemburg, engages to cause to be immediately converted into a Treaty with His Majesty the King of the Belgians, the Articles annexed to the present Act, and agreed upon by common consent, under the auspices of the Courts of Great Britain, Austria, France, Prussia, and Russia.

Article II. Her Majesty the Queen of the United Kingdom of Great Britain and Ireland, His Majesty the Emperor of Austria, King of Hungary and Bohemia, His Majesty the King of the French, His Majesty the King of Prussia, and His Majesty the Emperor of All the Russias, declare that the Articles mentioned in the preceding Article, are considered as having the same force and validity as if they were textually inserted in the present

Act, and that they are thus placed under the guarantee of their said Majesties.

Article III. The Union which has existed between Holland and Belgium, in virtue of the Treaty of Vienna of the 31st of May, 1815, is acknowledged by His Majesty the King of the Netherlands, Grand Duke of Luxemburg, to be dissolved.

ANNEX

*   *   *

Article VII. Belgium, within the limits specified in Articles I, II, and IV, shall form an Independent and perpetually Neutral State. It shall be bound to observe such Neutrality towards all other States.

42. Poland

(a) Article I of the Treaty of Vienna

Source: *British and Foreign State Papers*, II, 11, in Butterfield, p. 122.

The Duchy of Warsaw, saving those provinces and districts which have been otherwise disposed of in the following Articles, is joined to the Russian Empire. It shall be irrevocably attached to this Empire by its constitution, so as to be possessed by H.M. the Emperor of All the Russias, and his heirs and successors for ever. H.I.M. reserves the right to give this state, which shall have a separate administration, the internal development which he may think fit. He will adopt along with his other titles that of Tsar, King of Poland, according to the accustomed form which has been followed in the case of those titles which are attached to his other possessions.

Those Poles who [on the other hand] are the [direct] subjects of Russia, Austria and Prussia respectively, shall receive representative and national institutions adapted to that form of political life which each of the governments to which they belong shall judge useful and convenient to grant to them.

(b) The Revolt of 1830–32

The Poles appealed for recognition in a circular to the great European powers.

Source: *Annual Register*, 1831, pp. 415–17.

. . . An insurrection, distinguished for its energy and exemption from every excess, has severed the bonds which connected Poland with Russia. The kingdom is now subject only to a national government, unanimously chosen by a diet, the members of which, it is worthy of remark, were all elected under the Russian Government. That diet has entrusted the public affairs to persons the most eminent, both for birth and popularity, and whose political career affords the best guarantee to Europe. The diet has thus secured, in the strongest way possible, those monarchical institutions which the two Chambers have declared as best suited to the wishes and the wants of the nation. The national government of the Kingdom encounters no opposition in the exercise of its authority; its orders are executed with the utmost zeal, in every part of the Kingdom unoccupied by the enemy. The Polish troops, the armed representation of the opinions, of the desires, and of the power, of the nation, after three glorious, but deadly conflicts, after having sustained dreadful losses, have again completed their full numbers. . . .

If Belgium, which never ranked among states—if Greece, whose political existence has been annihilated for ages—have obtained, among all the uncertainty of war, the recognition of their independence, I ask if Poland has not stronger grounds for her pretensions. . . . The treaty of Vienna, when uniting the Kingdom of Poland to Russia, assured to us a national individuality, and a constitutional government. . . .

The Emperor of Russia has been the first to violate that treaty by overthrowing in the Kingdom the principal constitutional securities, in smothering all national spirit in the Polish provinces, in prohibiting even the use of our language. . . .

*   *   *

The revolt failed, and Tsar Nicholas I abolished the Constitution, 1832. This proclamation was followed by an Organic Statute, setting out the re-organisation of the State in detail.

Source: *British Parliamentary Papers*, XLVIII, in Robinson and Beard, p. 343.

When, by our manifesto of the 25th of January last year, we announced to our faithful subjects the entrance of our troops into the kingdom of Poland, which had been for a moment withdrawn by rebellion from the rule of its lawful sovereign, we at the same time declared our intention of establishing the future state of that country on a solid basis, in accordance with the wants and welfare of our whole empire. An end having now been put, by force of arms, to the disturbances by which the kingdom of Poland was agitated, and the nation, which had been led away by factious men, having been once more brought back to its duty and restored to tranquillity, we consider that the proper moment has come for carrying our intentions into execution, and for laying the foundation of a solid and lasting order of things, by which the peace and the indissoluble union of the two nations committed by Divine Providence to our care may be secured against every new attack.

*   *   *

. . . Torrents of blood have been shed. The tranquillity and happiness which the kingdom of Poland enjoyed in a degree that it had never before known, have been succeeded by the horrors of civil war and general desolation. But these misfortunes are now past. The kingdom of Poland, again restored to our dominion, is now at peace, and will again breathe under the auspices of a protecting government. But our paternal solicitude for our faithful subjects imposes upon us the duty of preventing, by all the means in our power, the return of similar disasters, by henceforward depriving the evil-disposed of the means which they have openly employed to disturb the public peace. . . .

Given at St. Petersburg the 14th (26th) February, in the year of our Lord 1832, and the seventh year of our reign.

(Signed) Nicholas
(Countersigned) Count Stephen Grabowski

43. Czechoslovakia: Masaryk's Confidential Memorandum, April 1915, on the Case for a New State

Jan Masaryk was the son of a coachman on a Hapsburg estate. He secured from the Allies the promise of independence and became President of the new state, 1918–39.

Source: R. W. Seton-Watson, *Masaryk in England* (1943), pp. 117–29.

Independent Bohemia: Prefatory Notice

This Memorandum gives the programme for the reorganisation of Bohemia as an independent State.

It is the programme of all Bohemian political parties except the Catholic Clericals. All details and minor problems are omitted. The plan of reconstructing the independent Bohemian State in the very heart of Europe naturally leads to the fundamental political problems of

the present war. The interdependence of all these problems explains why they are touched upon here, insofar as
the Bohemian and Slav questions seem to require it. . . .

[There follow paragraphs under nine headings analysing
these political problems of Europe.]

Austria, an Artificial State: Her Progressive Dismemberment

Austria, being an aggregate of nine small nations, is
quite an artificial State, as she was called by an Austrian
politician (Plener, the younger): no nation in Austria is so
populous that it would have the ruling majority. The
dynasty, therefore, tries to maintain its absolutistic position by the principle of *divide et impera,* by little conces-
sions now to one nation, now to another; the Germans
(the dynasty is German) and Magyars are the favourites.

Austria owes her origin to the invasions of the Turks,
and previously of the Huns (Magyars): Austria means the
Eastern Empire, the German provinces, Bohemia and
Hungary joined in a federation against Turkey.

With the fall of the Turks Austria falls also; Austria lost
her ruling idea, and is unable to find a positive idea.

So Austria falls from step to step. The Austrian-
Spanish Empire was dissolved. Austria lost the greater
part of Silesia and was driven by Prussia to abandon
Germany; in 1848, saved by Russia, she lost in 1859 the
Italian provinces; in 1866 she was beaten by Prussia.
Since then she exists only as the vassal of Berlin, being
divided into Austria and Hungary; it is to Berlin that both
the Germans and Magyars owe their dominating position
in Austria. . . .

[There follow paragraphs under these headings:
   Bohemia as part of Austria-Hungary.
   Bohemia forced to abandon Austria-Hungary.
   Bohemia for Russia, Serbia and the Allies.
   Bohemia claims her independence.]

CZECHOSLOVAKIA

The Independent Bohemian State:
Area and Population

The Bohemian State would be composed of the so-called Bohemian countries, namely of Bohemia, Moravia, Silesia; to these would be added the Slovak districts of North Hungary, from Ungvar through Kaschau along the ethnographical boundaries down the river Ipoly (Eipel) to the Danube, including Pressburg and the whole Slovak north to the frontier line of Hungary. The Slovaks are Bohemians, in spite of their using their dialect as their literary language. The Slovaks strive also for independence and accept the programme of union with Bohemia.

The Bohemian State would have a population of over 12 millions. The extent of the new state would be about 50,000 English square miles (Belgium has 11,373).

[Objections to the new state based on fear, and on the grounds of her size, poverty, and social set-up, are discussed.]

Possible objections to the creation of an Independent Bohemia

5. As it is not in our intention to hide the difficulties of Free Bohemia, we must mention the question of national minorities.

First, though we advocate the principle of nationality, we wish to retain our German minority. It seems to be a paradox, but it is on the principle of nationality that we retain the German minority. Bohemia is a quite unique example of a mixed country; in no country are two nationalities so intermixed and interwoven, so to say, as in Bohemia. Between the Germans and Italians, for instance, the ethnographical frontier is simple, sharply cut; it is not so in Bohemia—in a great many places, and in almost all the cities, we have Bohemian (or German) minorities.

[A paragraph: Bohemia not the only nation to be freed.]

Free Bohemia and Serbo-Croatia, as neighbouring Countries

The maximum of Bohemian and Serbo-Croatian wishes would be the connection of Bohemia and Serbo-Croatia.

This can be effected by giving the strip of land at the Hungarian frontier in the west either to Serbia or the half of it (north) to Bohemia, the other (south) to Serbia.

[Geographical, racial, and economic problems arising from this are discussed.]

44. The Ottoman Empire and the Eastern Question

(a) Greek War of Independence, 1821

The Greek National Assembly proclaimed Independence on 27 January 1822.

Source: *British & Foreign State Papers*, IX, 629 ff., in Robinson and Beard, pp. 384–6.

We, descendants of the wise and noble peoples of Hellas, we who are the contemporaries of the enlightened and civilized nations of Europe, we who behold the advantages which they enjoy under the protection of the impenetrable aegis of the law, find it no longer possible to suffer without cowardice and self-contempt the cruel yoke of the Ottoman power which has weighed upon us for more than four centuries,—a power which does not listen to reason and knows no other law than its own will, which orders and disposes everything despotically and according to its caprice. After this prolonged slavery we have determined to take arms to avenge ourselves and our country against a frightful tyranny, iniquitous in its very essence,—an un-exampled despotism to which no other rule can be compared.

The war which we are carrying on against the Turk is not that of a faction or the result of sedition. It is not aimed at the advantage of any single part of the Greek people; it is a national war, a holy war, a war the object of which is to reconquer the rights of individual liberty, of property and honour,—rights which the civilized people of Europe, our neighbours, enjoy today; rights of which the cruel and unheard-of tyranny of the Ottomans would deprive us,—us alone,—and the very memory of which they would stifle in our hearts.

Are we, then, less reasonable than other peoples, that we remain deprived of these rights? Are we of a nature so degraded and abject that we should be viewed as unworthy to enjoy them, condemned to remain crushed under a perpetual slavery and subjected, like beasts of burden or mere automatons, to the absurd caprice of a cruel tyrant who, like an infamous brigand, has come from distant regions to invade our borders? Nature has deeply graven these rights in the hearts of all men; laws in harmony with nature have so completely consecrated them that neither three nor four centuries—nor thousands nor millions of centuries—can destroy them. Force and violence have been able to restrict and paralyse them for a season, but force may once more resuscitate them in all the vigour which they formerly enjoyed during many centuries; nor have we ever ceased in Hellas to defend these rights by arms whenever opportunity offered.

Building upon the foundation of our natural rights, and desiring to assimilate ourselves to the rest of the Christians of Europe, our brethren, we have begun a war against the Turks, or rather, uniting all our isolated strength, we have formed ourselves into a single armed body, firmly resolved to attain our end, to govern ourselves by wise laws, or to be altogether annihilated, believing it to be unworthy of us, as descendants of the glorious peoples of Hellas, to live henceforth in a state of slavery fitted rather for unreasoning animals than for rational beings.

Ten months have elapsed since we began this national

war; the all-powerful God has succoured us; although we were not adequately prepared for so great an enterprise, our arms have everywhere been victorious, despite the powerful obstacles which we have encountered and still encounter everywhere. We have had to contend with a situation bristling with difficulties, and we are still engaged in our efforts to overcome them. It should not therefore appear astonishing that we were not able from the very first to proclaim our independence and take rank among the civilized peoples of the earth, marching forward side by side with them. It was impossible to occupy ourselves with our political existence before we had established our independence. We trust these reasons may justify, in the eyes of the nations, our delay, as well as console us for the anarchy in which we have found ourselves. . . .

Epidaurus, January 15/27, 1822:
the First Year of Independence.
A. Mavrocordato, President of the National Assembly.

(b) Russian Aims in the Balkans, 1877

The following proclamation to the Bulgarians, 28 June 1877, by Tsar Alexander II reveals both Russian idealism and Russian desire to expand her influence.

Source: E. Herslet, IV, p. 2640, in Robinson and Beard, p. 395.

My troops, having crossed the Danube, will today enter your territory upon which they have already fought more than once for the amelioration of the condition of the Christian inhabitants of the Balkan Peninsula. My ancestors, faithful to their ancient and historical traditions, ever gathering fresh strength from the intimate union which had for centuries united them to the orthodox population, succeeded, by their influence and their arms, in securing the present position of the Servians and the

Roumanians by summoning them to a new political existence. Time and circumstances have not altered the sympathies of Russia for her co-religionists in the East. She nourishes ever the same affection, the same solicitude towards all the members of the great Christian family of the Balkan Peninsula. . . .

Inhabitants of Bulgaria! The aim of Russia is to build up, not to destroy. She is called by the decrees of Providence to pacify and conciliate all races and all denominations in the Bulgarian territory, which is inhabited by people of various origin and belief. Henceforward the arms of Russia will protect all Christians against violence of all kind; no attack will be made by anyone with impunity upon either their persons or their property; every crime will be followed by punishment; the life, liberty, honour and property of every Christian will be equally guaranteed, to whatever sect he may belong. Vengeance will not guide our actions; a sentiment of strict equity will alone preside over them, as well as the firm intention of developing order and law in regions where disorder and despotism are now rampant.

And to you, Mussulmans of Bulgaria, I address a salutary warning. It is painful for me to evoke the memory of the crimes and violence of which many of you have been guilty toward defenceless Christians. These horrors cannot be forgotten, but the Russian authorities do not wish to hold all responsible for the crimes of a few. A regular and impartial administration of justice will overtake only the criminals who have remained unpunished, although their names were perfectly well known to our government. Recognize today that it is the justice of God which overtakes you; bend before his will; submit yourselves to the lawful demands of the authorities who will be appointed whenever my troops appear; become peaceful citizens of a society which is ready to accord to you the benefits of a regular organization. Your religion will remain to you intact; your existence, your property, the life and property of your families, will be held sacred by us.

Christians of Bulgaria! You are passing through a memorable period. The hour of deliverance from Mussulman despotism has at length struck. Give the world an illustration of Christian love; forget former internal dissensions, and respect scrupulously the legitimate rights of each nationality; unite yourselves, as brothers in religion, in a sentiment of concord and brotherly love, which alone offers foundations for a solid and lasting edifice; gather closely under the shadow of the Russian flag, whose victories have so often resounded upon the Danube and among the Balkans. As the Russian troops advance into the interior of the country, the Turkish rule will be replaced by a regular organization, the native inhabitants will be at once summoned to take an active part therein under the supreme direction of special and newly appointed authorities. Obey the Russian authorities. Follow their directions faithfully. Therein lies your strength and your safety.

With humility I beseech the Lord to grant us the victory over the enemy of the Christians, and to send down his blessing upon our just cause.

Alexander

(c) The Congress of Berlin, 1878

The following are some of the more important clauses of the treaty of 1878.

Source: E. Herslet, pp. 2764 ff., in Robinson and Beard, p. 396.

Art. 1. Bulgaria is constituted an autonomous and tributary principality under the suzerainty of his Imperial Majesty the Sultan; it shall have a Christian government and a national militia.

Art. 2. [Defines its extent].

*   *   *

Art. 13. A province shall be formed south of the Balkans which shall take the name of 'Eastern Roumelia', and shall remain under the direct political and military authority of his Imperial Majesty the Sultan, under conditions of administrative autonomy. It shall have a Christian governor general.

* * *

Art. 25. The provinces of Bosnia and Herzegovina shall be occupied and administered by Austria-Hungary.

Art. 26. The independence of Montenegro is recognized by the Sublime Porte and by all of those high contracting parties who have not hitherto admitted it.

* * *

Art. 34. The high contracting parties recognize the independence of the Principality of Servia, subject to the conditions set forth in the following article [on civil and religious liberty] . . .

* * *

Art. 43. The high contracting parties recognize the independence of Roumania subject to the conditions set forth in the two following articles [on civil and religious liberty] . . .

* * *

Art. 58. The Sublime Porte cedes to the Russian emperor in Asia the territories of Ardahan, Kars, and Batum, together with the latter port, as well as all the territories comprised between the former Russo-Turkish frontier and the following line [drawn roughly about forty miles to the south of the old Russian boundary].

* * *

Art. 62. The Sublime Porte having expressed the intention to maintain the principle of religious liberty [16] and

[16] In a decree issued in 1856.

give it the widest scope, the contracting parties take note of this spontaneous declaration. In no part of the Ottoman Empire shall difference of religion be alleged against any person as a ground for exclusion or incapacity as regards the discharge of civil and political rights, admission to the public employments, functions, and honours, or the exercise of the various professions and industries. All persons shall be admitted without distinction of religion to give evidence before the tribunals. The freedom and outward exercise of all forms of worship are assured to all. . . .

(d) The Allied Entry into Jerusalem, 1917

Source: *The Times*, 13 December 1917.

THE ENTRY INTO JERUSALEM.
PROCESSION ON FOOT.
PROCLAMATION TO THE INHABITANTS.

The following telegram, received yesterday from General Sir E. Allenby, was read in the House of Commons by Mr. Lloyd George.

Jerusalem—2 p.m. Dec. 11. 1917.

I entered this city officially at noon today with a few of my staff, the commanders of the French and Italian detachments and the Military Attachés of France, Italy and the U.S.A.

The procession was all on foot. At the Jaffa Gate I was received by guards representing England, Scotland, Ireland, Wales, Australia, New Zealand, India, France and Italy. The population received me well. Guards have been placed over the Holy Places. My Military Governor is in touch with the acting Custos of the Latins and the Greek representative. The Governor has detailed an officer to supervise Christian Holy Places. The following proclamation was read in my presence to the population in Arabic,

Hebrew, English, French, Italian, Greek and Russian, from the steps of the Citadel.

Proclamation of martial law in Jerusalem.

To the inhabitants of Jerusalem the Blessed and the people dwelling in the vicinity. The defeat inflicted upon the Turks by the troops under my command has resulted in the occupation of your city by my forces. I therefore proclaim it to be under martial law . . . it is my desire that every person should pursue his lawful business without fear of interruption.

Furthermore, since your city is regarded with affection by the adherents of three of the great religions of mankind, and its soil has been consecrated by the prayers and pilgrimages of multitudes of devout people of those three religions for many centuries, therefore do I make known to you that every sacred building, monument, Holy Spot, Shrine, traditional site, endowment, pious bequest or customary place of prayer, of whatsoever form of the three religions will be protected according to the existing customs and beliefs of those to whose faiths they are sacred.

Letter to King George V from the Chief Rabbi, Dr. Hertz, 11 December 1917.

Source: *The Times*, 14 December 1917.

On behalf of the Jewish communities of the Empire . . . I humbly beg to congratulate Your Majesty on the world historic victories in the Holy Land.

The occupation of Jerusalem, following so closely upon the epoch making Declaration of Your Majesty's government on Palestine as the national home for the Jewish people[17] causes the hearts of millions of my brethren to throb with deepest gratitude to Almighty God who alone doeth wondrous things. The House of Israel, that for

[17] The Balfour Declaration, 1 November 1917.

2,500 years preferred Jerusalem above its chief joy, fervently prays that everywhere the heroic efforts of Your Majesty's forces may be speedily crowned with complete and lasting success.

45. The Papacy: Decree of Papal Infallibility, 1870

The Papacy lost its temporal possessions to the new kingdom of Italy, but its spiritual authority remained. The Decree of Papal Infallibility of 1870 was the culmination of a long movement in the Church.

Source: C. Mirbt, *Quellen zur Geschichte des Papsttums und des römischen Katholizismus*, pp. 465–6, tr. in Butterfield, p. 144.

We, therefore, faithfully keeping to the tradition that has come down to us from the beginning of the Catholic faith, and working for the glory of God our Saviour, the exaltation of the Catholic religion, and the salvation of the people of Christ, do with the approval of the Holy Council teach and define as a divinely-revealed dogma: that the Roman Pontiff, when he speaks ex cathedra, that is to say, when he discharges the office of Pastor and Teacher of all Christians by defining in virtue of his supreme Apostolic authority a doctrine regarding faith or morals to be held by the universal church, is by the divine assistance promised to him in Blessed Peter possessed of that infallibility which the Divine Redeemer wished to bestow upon His Church for the definition of doctrine in regard to faith or morals; and that therefore such definitions by the Roman Pontiff are in their nature, apart from the consent of the Church, irreformable.

But if anyone presume to contradict this our definition —which may God avert—let him be anathema.

Intellectual and General

In this section are a few extracts illustrating some of the main political ideas and hopes of the period. It is clearly incomplete—for instance, it was impossible to give, in short extracts, an accurate illustration of the scientific, psychological, and technological changes which are so important in the period.

46. The Idea of Progress: Robert Owen (1771–1858), Writing in 1841

This extract from the English manufacturer, social reformer, and socialist, reflects the optimism of secular, scientific man, and develops one of the most frequent criticisms made of nineteenth century capitalism.

Source: R. Owen, *A Development of the Principles and Plan on which to Establish Self Supporting Home Colonies* (1841), pp. 11, 22 ff.

The almost miraculous decline of reverence for the priesthood over the world;—their insane dissensions in opposition to each other, and, at this stage of society, their equally insane presumption over their more enlightened fellow-men;—the progress of the temperance societies in Great Britain and America; the daily advance of scientific discoveries; the new passion for educating the masses; the extraordinary disinclination to war among the British and other warlike nations; the easy and rapid communication between the most distant countries; the general adoption by civilized countries of scientific power to supersede the necessity for severe or injurious manual service; and the friendly union of governments which until latterly have been in a great savage hostility to each other;—all, with many other strange and extraordinary occurring events, indicate with unerring certainty that a great change is coming over the nations of the earth; and that the wise, the good, the happy existence of man approaches with gigantic strides; in fact, that the millennium is not far distant.

And shall irrational man, in any of his present puerile divisions of class, or sect, or party, or country, or colour, set himself to oppose this great, magnificent, and glorious change for the benefit of the human race now and through the coming ages? Vain and useless will such attempts prove. The decree has gone forth from the almighty energies of the universe, that man shall be put in the right path now, to become good and wise and happy; and every obstacle in the way of his progress to this advent of his existence shall prove unavailing and powerless. . . .

But to effect this great and glorious change, it must be made known to the world: . . .

[There follows an attack on (1) the Law, on (2) the profession of arms, and (3) on the competition system.]

That the necessary character of the individual buying-and-selling system is to train the human race to acquire the inferior mind of a pedlar and dealer whose business of life is to endeavour to procure everything from others at the lowest price and to dispose of everything to others at the highest price, or in such a manner that he shall secure the greatest amount of money, profit, worldly honours, or individual considerations to himself. And in this sense, all, from the highest to the lowest, are now trained to become, by the individual competition system, mere pedlars, tradesmen, or dealers, who are constantly endeavouring to obtain the services and productions of others at the easiest rate, the lowest value, and to sell their own services at the highest, or to obtain all they can in exchange for them. The sovereigns, statesmen, legislators, professional men, military, merchants, bankers, manufacturers, tradesmen, workmen, and beggars are now all, under the individual competitive system which has hitherto prevailed over the world, engaged in this low, unjust, degrading traffic. . . . By these means the successful in this inferior and immoral course of conduct do not obtain a tithe, no, nor a fiftieth part of the permanent, substantial, healthy, enlightened, superior advantages, pleasures, and enjoyments that, under the united system, *all* may attain and securely possess without obstruction, competition, or contest.

47. The Communist Manifesto of Marx and Engels, 1848 (condensed)

Source: *The Communist Manifesto*, Eden and Cedar Paul (1930).

A spectre haunts Europe—the spectre of Communism. All the powers of old Europe have entered into a holy alliance in order to lay this spectre: Pope and Tsar; Metternich and Guizot, French radicals and German police.

* * *

I. BOURGEOIS AND PROLETARIANS

The history of all human society, past and present, has been the history of class struggles.

Freeman and slave, patrician and plebeian, baron and serf, guild-burgess and journeyman—in a word, oppressor and oppressed—stood in sharp opposition to each other. They carried on perpetual warfare, sometimes masked, sometimes open and acknowledged. . . .

Our own age, the bourgeois age, is distinguished by this—that it has simplified class antagonisms. More and more, society is splitting into two great hostile camps, into two great and directly contraposed classes: bourgeoisie and proletariat.

[The rise of the bourgeoisie is traced from the towns of the Middle Ages, through the expansion of world markets and the Industrial Revolution.]

Wherever the bourgeoisie has risen to power, it has destroyed all feudal, patriarchal and idyllic relationships. It has ruthlessly torn asunder the motley feudal ties that bound men to their 'natural superiors'; it has left no other bond betwixt man and man but crude self interest and un-feeling cash payment. . . .

The bourgeoisie has robbed of their haloes various occupations hitherto regarded with awe and veneration. Doctor, lawyer, priest, poet and scientist, have become its wage labourers.

The bourgeoisie has torn the veil of sentiment from the family relationship which has become an affair of money and nothing more.

[The vast expansion of production under the bourgeoisie has become world wide, destroying national self-dependence and creating economic problems of over-production.]

The weapons with which the bourgeoisie overthrew feudalism are now being turned against the bourgeoisie itself.

But the bourgeoisie has not only forged the weapons that will slay it; it has also engendered the men who will use these weapons—the modern workers, the PROLE-TARIANS.

*   *   *

. . . The worker has become a mere appendage to a machine; a person from whom nothing but the simplest, the most monotonous, and the most easily learned manipulations are expected. The cost of production of a worker therefore amounts to little more than the cost of the means of subsistence he needs for his upkeep and for the propagation of his race. . . .

Modern industry has transformed the little workshop of the patriarchal master into the huge factory of the industrial capitalist. Masses of workers, crowded together in the factory, are organised in military fashion. . . . They are not merely the slaves of the bourgeois class, of the bourgeois State; they are in daily and hourly thraldom to the machine, to the foreman, and above all, to the individual bourgeois manufacturer. . . .

[The organization of workers' resistance has developed culminating in the class conscious, belligerent proletariat.]

II

[Various criticisms of Communism are discussed and dismissed as expressions of bourgeois self-interest.]

Enough of these bourgeois objections to Communism! . . . We have already seen that the first step in the workers' revolution is to make the workers the ruling class, to establish democracy.

The proletariat will use its political supremacy in order, by degrees, to wrest all capital from the bourgeoisie, to centralise all the means of production into the hands of the State (this meaning the proletariat organised as the ruling class) and as rapidly as possible to increase the total mass of productive forces. . . .

* * *

In the most advanced countries they [Communist measures] will, generally speaking, take the following forms:

1. Expropriation of landed property, and the use of land rents to defray State expenditure.

2. A vigorously graduated income tax.

3. Abolition of the right of inheritance.

*   *   *

5. Centralisation of credit in the hands of the State, by means of a national bank with State capital and an exclusive monopoly.

6. Centralisation of the means of transport in the hands of the State.

7. Increase of national factories and means of production, cultivation of uncultivated land, and improvement of cultivated land in accordance with a general plan.

8. Universal and equal obligation to work, organisation of industrial armies, especially for agriculture.

*   *   *

10. Public and free education of all children. Abolition of factory work for children in its present form. Education and material production to be combined.

*   *   *

The old bourgeois society, with its classes and class conflicts, will be replaced by an association in which the free development of each will lead to the free development of all.

[Section III follows, in which various other forms of 'socialism' are criticized. Section IV explains the attitude of Communists towards other opposition parties, and:]

. . . Communists scorn to hide their views and aims. They openly declare that their purposes can only be achieved by the forcible overthrow of the whole extant social order. Let the ruling classes tremble at the prospect of a communist revolution. Proletarians have nothing to lose but their chains. They have a world to win. PRO-LETARIANS OF ALL LANDS, UNITE!

48. Disarmament: Tsar Nicholas II's Appeal, 1898

The first international Peace Conference was held the following year at The Hague, a second in 1907.

Source: Holls, *The Peace Congress at The Hague*, pp. 18 ff., in Robinson and Beard, pp. 463-5.

The maintenance of general peace, and a possible reduction of the excessive armaments which weigh upon all nations, present themselves in the existing condition of the whole world, as the ideal towards which the endeavours of all governments should be directed.

The humanitarian and magnanimous ideas of His Majesty the Emperor, my august master, have been won over to this view. In the conviction that this lofty aim is in conformity with the most essential interests and the legitimate views of all powers, the Imperial Government thinks that the present moment would be very favourable for seeking, by means of international discussion, the most effectual means of insuring to all peoples the benefits of a real and durable peace, and, above all, of putting an end to the progressive development of the present armaments.

In the course of the last twenty years the longings for a general pacification have become especially pronounced in the consciences of civilized nations. The preservation of peace has been put forward as the object of international policy; in its name great States have concluded powerful alliances between themselves. It is the better to guarantee peace that they have developed, in proportions hitherto unprecedented, their military forces, and still continue to increase them without shrinking from any sacrifice.

All these efforts, nevertheless, have not yet been able to

bring about the beneficent results of the desired pacification. The financial burdens following an upward trend
strike the public prosperity at its very source.

The intellectual and physical strength of the nations,
labour and capital, are, for the major part, diverted from
their natural application and unproductively consumed.
Hundreds of millions are devoted to acquiring terrible
engines of destruction, which, though today regarded as
the last word of science, are destined tomorrow to lose all
value in consequence of some fresh discovery in the same
field.

National culture, economic progress, and the production
of wealth are either paralysed or checked in their development. Moreover, in proportion as the armaments of
each power increase, so do they less and less fulfil the
object which the governments have set before themselves.

The economic crises, due in great part to the system of
armaments à l'outrance, and the continual danger which
lies in this massing of war material, are transforming the
armed peace of our days into a crushing burden, which the
peoples have more and more difficulty in bearing. It
appears evident, then, that if this state of things be prolonged, it will inevitably lead to the very cataclysm which
it is desired to avert, and the horrors of which make every
thinking man shudder in advance.

To put an end to these incessant armaments and to seek
the means of warding off the calamities which are threaten-
ing the whole world,—such is the supreme duty which is
today imposed on all States.

Filled with this idea, his Majesty has been pleased to
order me to propose to all the governments whose representatives are accredited to the Imperial Court, the meeting of a conference which should occupy itself with this
grave problem.

This conference should be, by the help of God, a happy

presage for the century which is about to open. It would converge in one powerful focus the efforts of all States which are sincerely seeking to make the great idea of universal peace triumph over the elements of trouble and discord.

It would, at the same time, confirm their agreement by the solemn establishment of the principles of justice and right, upon which repose the security of States and the welfare of peoples.

49. The Great War, 1914–18: Attitudes

Crowds welcomed the outbreak of war on both sides. These two poems, from the English side, show the change of mood. Both poets saw action: Brooke died en route to the Middle East and Owen was killed in battle on the Western Front.

Source: *The Collected Poems of Rupert Brooke.*

The Dead

Blow out, you bugles, over the rich Dead!
There's none of these so lonely and poor of old,
But, dying, has made us rarer gifts than gold.
These laid the world away; poured out the red
Sweet wine of youth; gave up the years to be
Of work and joy, and that unhoped serene,
That men call age; and those who would have been,
Their sons, they gave, their immortality.

Blow, bugles, blow! They brought us, for our dearth,
Holiness, lacked so long, and Love, and Pain.
Honour has come back, as a king, to earth,
And paid his subjects with a royal wage;
And Nobleness walks in our ways again;
And we have come into our heritage.

Rupert Brooke

Source: *The Poems of Wilfred Owen.*

Dulce et Decorum Est

Bent double, like old beggars under sacks,
Knock-kneed, coughing like hags, we cursed through
    sludge,
Till on the haunting flares we turned our backs,
And towards our distant rest began to trudge.
Men marched asleep. Many had lost their boots,
But limped on, blood-shod. All went lame, all blind;
Drunk with fatigue; deaf even to the hoots
Of gas-shells dropping softly behind.
Gas! Gas! Quick, boys!—An ecstasy of fumbling,
Fitting the clumsy helmets just in time,
But someone still was yelling out and stumbling
And floundering like a man in fire or lime.—
Dim through the misty panes and thick green light,
As under a green sea, I saw him drowning.

In all my dreams before my helpless sight
He plunges at me, guttering, choking, drowning.
If in some smothering dreams, you too could pace
Behind the wagon that we flung him in,
And watch the white eyes writhing in his face,
His hanging face, like a devil's sick of sin;
If you could hear, at every jolt, the blood
Come gargling from the froth-corrupted lungs,
Bitter as the cud
Of vile, incurable sores on innocent tongues,—
My friend, you would not tell with such high zest
To children ardent for some desperate glory,
The old lie: Dulce et decorum est
Pro patria mori.

Wilfred Owen

50. American Intervention: President Wilson's War Message, 2 April 1917

Source: *The Congressional Record.*

Gentlemen of the Congress: I have called the Congress into extraordinary session because there are serious, very serious choices of policy to be made, and made immediately which it was neither right nor constitutionally permissible that I should assume the responsibility of making.

On the third of February last, I officially laid before you the extraordinary announcement of the Imperial German Government that on and after the first day of February it was its purpose to put aside all restraints of law or of humanity and use its submarines to sink every vessel that sought to approach either the ports of Great Britain and Ireland or the western coast of Europe or any of the ports controlled by the enemies of Germany within the Mediterranean. . . .

. . . The new policy has swept every restriction aside. Vessels of every kind, whatever their flag, their character, their cargo, their destination, their errand, have been ruthlessly sent to the bottom without warning and without thought of help or mercy for those on board—the vessels of friendly neutrals along with those of belligerents. Even hospital ships and ships carrying relief to the sorely bereaved and stricken people of Belgium, though the latter were provided with safe conduct through the proscribed areas by the German Government itself, and were distinguished by unmistakable marks of identity, have been sunk with the same reckless lack of compassion or of principle.

* * *

With a profound sense of the solemn and even tragical character of the step I am taking and of the grave responsibilities which it involves, but in unhesitating obedience to what I deem my constitutional duty, I advise that the Congress declare the recent course of the Imperial German Government to be, in fact, nothing less than war against the Government and people of the United States; that it formally accept the status of belligerent which has thus been thrust upon it; and that it take immediate steps not only to put the country in a more thorough state of defense, but also to exert all its power and employ all its resources to bring the Government of the German Empire to terms and end the war.

*　　*　　*

We have no quarrel with the German people. We have no feeling toward them but one of sympathy and friendship. It was not upon their impulse that their Government acted in entering this war. It was not with their previous knowledge or approval.

It was a war determined upon as wars used to be determined upon in the old, unhappy days when peoples were nowhere consulted by their rulers and wars were provoked and waged in the interest of dynasties or of little groups of ambitious men who were accustomed to use their fellow-men as pawns and tools.

Self-governed nations do not fill their neighbor states with spies or set the course of intrigue to bring about some critical posture of affairs which will give them an opportunity to strike and make conquest. Such designs can be successfully worked out only under cover and where no one has the right to ask questions.

Cunningly contrived plans of deception or aggression, carried, it may be, from generation to generation, can be worked out and kept from the light only within the privacy of courts or behind the carefully guarded confidences of a narrow and privileged class. They are happily impossible where public opinion commands and insists upon full information concerning all the nation's affairs.

* * *

Does not every American feel that assurance has been added to our hope for the future peace of the world by the wonderful and heartening things that have been happening within the last few weeks in Russia?

* * *

. . . It is a distressing and oppressive duty, gentlemen of the Congress, which I have performed in thus addressing you. There are, it may be, many months of fiery trial and sacrifice ahead of us. It is a fearful thing to lead this great peaceful people into war, into the most terrible and disastrous of all wars, civilization itself seeming to be in the balance. But the right is more precious than peace, and we shall fight for the things which we have always carried nearest our hearts—for democracy, for the right of those who submit to authority to have a voice in their own governments, for the rights and liberties of small nations, for a universal domination of right by such a concert of free peoples as shall bring peace and safety to all nations and make the world itself at last free. To such a task we can dedicate our lives and our fortunes, everything that we are and everything that we have, with the pride of those who know that the day has come when America is privileged to spend her blood and her might for the principles that gave her birth and happiness and the peace which she has treasured. God helping her, she can do no other.

WOODROW WILSON

51. The Signing of the Peace of Versailles, 1919

Harold Nicolson helped to draft the Treaty.

Source: Sir Harold Nicolson, *Peacemaking 1919* (1937 ed.), pp. 365–70.

June 28, Saturday.

*　　*　　*

There is no crowd at all until we reach Ville d'Avray. But there are poilus at every crossroad waving red flags and stopping all other traffic. When we reach Versailles the crowd thickens. The avenue up to the Chateau is lined with cavalry in steel-blue helmets. The pennants of their lances flutter red and white in the sun. In the Cour d'Honneur, from which the captured German cannon have tactfully been removed, are further troops. There are Generals, Pétain, Gouraud, Mangin. There are St. Cyriens. Very military and orderly. Headlam Morley and I creep out of our car hurriedly. Feeling civilian and grubby. And wholly unimportant. We hurry through the door.

Magnificent upon the staircase stand the Gardes Ré-publicains—two caryatides on every step—their sabres at the salute. This is a great ordeal, but there are other people climbing the stairs with us. . . .

*　　*　　*

We enter the Galerie des Glaces. It is divided into three sections. At the far end are the Press already thickly in-stalled. In the middle there is a horse-shoe table for the plenipotentiaries. In front of that, like a guillotine, is the table for the signatures. It is supposed to be raised on a dais but, if so, the dais can be but a few inches high. In the nearer distance are rows and rows of tabourets for the distinguished guests, the deputies, the senators and the members of the delegations. There must be seats for over a thousand persons. This robs the ceremony of all privilege and therefore of all dignity. It is like the Aeolian Hall.

Clemenceau is already seated under the heavy ceiling as we arrive. 'Le roi,' runs the scroll above him, 'gouverne par lui-même.' He looks small and yellow. A crunched homunculus.

Conversation clatters out among the mixed groups around us. It is, as always on such occasions, like water running into a tin bath. . . .

People step over the Aubusson benches and escabeaux to talk to friends. Meanwhile the delegates arrive in little bunches and push up the central aisle slowly. Wilson and Lloyd George are among the last. They take their seats at the central table. The table is at last full. Clemenceau glances to right and left. People sit down upon their escabeaux but continue chattering. Clemenceau makes a sign to the ushers. They say 'Sssh! Sssh! Ssh!' People cease chattering and there is only the sound of occasional coughing and the dry rustle of programmes. The officials of the Protocol of the Foreign Office move up the aisle and say 'Sssh! Sssh!' again. There is then an absolute hush, followed by a sharp military order. The Gardes Républicains at the doorway flash their swords into their scabbards with a loud click. 'Faites entrer les Allemands,' says Clemenceau in the ensuing silence. His voice is distant but harshly penetrating. A hush follows.

Through the door at the end appear two huissiers with silver chains. They march in single file. After them come four officers of France, Great Britain, America and Italy. And then, isolated and pitiable, come the two German delegates, Dr. Müller, Dr. Bell. The silence is terrifying. Their feet upon a strip of parquet between the savonnerie carpets echo hollow and duplicate. They keep their eyes fixed away from those two thousand staring eyes, fixed upon the ceiling. They are deathly pale. They do not appear as representatives of a brutal militarism. The one is thin and pink-eyelidded: the second fiddle in a Brunswick orchestra. The other is moon-faced and suffering: a privat-dozent. It is all most painful.

They are conducted to their chairs. Clemenceau at once breaks the silence. 'Messieurs,' he rasps' 'la séance est ouverte.' He adds a few ill-chosen words. 'We are here to sign a Treaty of Peace.' The Germans leap up anxiously when he has finished, since they know that they are the first to sign. William Martin, as if a theatre manager, motions them petulantly to sit down again. Mantoux translates Clemenceau's words into English. Then St. Quentin advances towards the Germans and with the utmost dignity leads them to the little table on which the Treaty is expanded. There is general tension. They sign. There is a general relaxation. Conversation hums again in an undertone. The delegates stand up one by one and pass onwards to the queue which waits by the signature table. Meanwhile people buzz round the main table getting autographs. The single file of plenipotentiaries waiting to approach the table gets thicker. It goes quickly. The officials of the Quai d'Orsay stand round, indicating places to sign, indicating procedure, blotting with neat little pads.

Suddenly from outside comes the crash of guns thundering a salute. It announces to Paris that the second Treaty of Versailles has been signed by Dr. Müller and Dr. Bell. Through the few open windows comes the sound of distant crowds cheering hoarsely. And still the signature goes on.

We had been warned it might last three hours. Yet almost at once it seemed that the queue was getting thin. Only three, then two, and then one delegate remained to sign. His name had hardly been blotted before the huissiers began again their 'Sssh! Ssh!' cutting suddenly short the wide murmur which had again begun. There was a final hush. 'La séance est levée,' rasped Clemenceau. Not a word more or less.

We kept our seats while the Germans were conducted like prisoners from the dock, their eyes still fixed upon some distant point of the horizon.

We still kept our seats to allow the Big Five to pass down the aisle. Wilson, Lloyd George, the Dominions, others. Finally, Clemenceau, with his rolling satirical gait. Painlevé, who was sitting one off me, rose to greet him. He stretched out both his hands and grasped Clemenceau's right glove. He congratulated him. 'Oui,' says Clemenceau, 'c'est une belle journée.' There were tears in his bleary eyes.

Marie Murat was near me and had overhead. 'En êtes-vous sûre?' I ask her. 'Pas du tout,' she answers, being a woman of intelligence.

*   *   *

52. The Covenant of the League of Nations, 1919

Source: H. W. V. Temperley, *A History of the Peace Conference of Paris* (1920–24), III, 111–23.

The High Contracting Parties,
   In order to promote international co-operation and to achieve international peace and security

> by the acceptance of obligations not to resort to war,
> by the prescription of open, just and honourable relations between nations,
> by the firm establishment of the understandings of international law as the actual rule of conduct among Governments, and

by the maintenance of justice and a scrupulous respect for all treaty obligations in the dealings of organized peoples with one another,

Agree to this Covenant of the League of Nations . . .

Art. 2. The action of the League under this Covenant shall be effected through the instrumentality of an Assembly and of a Council, with a permanent Secretariat. . . .

Art. 8. The Members of the League recognize that the maintenance of peace requires the reduction of national armaments to the lowest point consistent with national safety and the enforcement by common action of international obligations. . . .

* * *

Art. 11. Any war or threat of war, whether immediately affecting any of the Members of the League or not, is hereby declared a matter of concern to the whole League, and the League shall take any action that may be deemed wise and effectual to safeguard the peace of nations. In case any such emergency should arise the Secretary-General shall on the request of any Member of the League forthwith summon a meeting of the Council.

It is also declared to be the friendly right of each Member of the League to bring to the attention of the Assembly or of the Council any circumstance whatever affecting international relations which threatens to disturb international peace or the good understanding between nations upon which peace depends.

Art. 12. The Members of the League agree that if there should arise between them any dispute likely to lead to a rupture, they will submit the matter either to arbitration or to inquiry by the Council, and they agree in no case to resort to war until three months after the award by the arbitrators or the report by the Council. . . .

* * *

Art. 14. The Council shall formulate and submit to Members of the League for adoption plans for the establishment of a Permanent Court of International Justice. The Court shall be competent to hear and determine any dispute of an international character which the parties thereto submit to it. The Court may also give an advisory opinion upon any dispute or question referred to it by the Council or by the Assembly.

* * *

Art. 16. Should any Member of the League resort to war in disregard of its covenants under Articles 12, 13 or 15, it shall ipso facto be deemed to have committed an act of war against all other Members of the League, which hereby undertake immediately to subject it to the severance of all trade or financial relations, the prohibition of all intercourse between their nationals and the nationals of the covenant-breaking State, and the prevention of all financial, commercial or personal intercourse between the nationals of the covenant-breaking State and the nationals of any other State, whether a Member of the League or not.

It shall be the duty of the Council in such case to recommend to the several Governments concerned what effective military, naval or air force the Members of the League shall severally contribute to the armed forces to be used to protect the covenants of the League.

The Members of the League agree, further, that they will mutually support one another in the financial and economic measures which are taken under this Article, in order to minimize the loss and inconvenience resulting from the above measures and that they will mutually support one another in resisting any special measures aimed at one of their number by the covenant-breaking State, and that they will take the necessary steps to afford passage through their territory to the forces of any of the Members of the League which are co-operating to protect the covenants of the League. . . .

*　　*　　*

Art. 18. Every treaty or international engagement entered into hereafter by any Member of the League shall be forthwith registered with the Secretariat and shall as soon as possible be published by it. No such treaty or international engagement shall be binding until so registered.

Art. 22. To those colonies and territories which as a consequence of the late war have ceased to be under the sovereignty of the States which formerly governed them and which are inhabited by peoples not yet able to stand by themselves under the strenuous conditions of the modern world, there should be applied the principle that the wellbeing and development of such peoples form a sacred trust of civilization and that securities for the performance of this trust should be embodied in this Covenant.

The best method of giving practical effect to this principle is that the tutelage of such peoples should be entrusted to advanced nations who by reason of their resources, their experience or their geographical position can best undertake this responsibility, and who are willing to accept it, and that this tutelage should be exercised by them as Mandatories on behalf of the League.

The character of the mandate must differ according to the stage of the development of the people, the geographical situation of the territory, its economic conditions and other similar circumstances.

[Here follow definitions of different kinds of mandate.]

In every case of mandate, the Mandatory shall render to the Council an annual report in reference to the territory committed to its charge.

Art. 23. Subject to and in accordance with the provisions of international conventions existing or hereafter to be agreed upon, the Members of the League:

(*a*) will endeavour to secure and maintain fair and humane conditions of labour for men, women and children, both in their own countries and in all countries to which their commercial and industrial relations extend, and for that purpose will establish and maintain the necessary international organizations;

(*b*) undertake to secure just treatment of the native inhabitants of territories under their control;

(*c*) will entrust the League with the general supervision over the execution of agreements with regard to the traffic in women and children, and the traffic in opium and other dangerous drugs;

(*d*) will entrust the League with the general supervision of the trade in arms and ammunition with the countries in which the control of this traffic is necessary in the common interest;

(*e*) will make provision to secure and maintain freedom of communications and of transit and equitable treatment for the commerce of all Members of the League. In this connection, the special necessities of the regions devastated during the war of 1914–1918 shall be borne in mind;

(*f*) will endeavour to take steps in matters of international concern for the prevention and control of disease.

53. The Great Slump, 1929–33

The collapse on Wall Street was only one factor, part cause and part effect; these brief extracts from *The Times* make clear the dramatic and uncertain course of events:

THE GREAT SLUMP, 1929–33

WALL STREET PANIC—
RECORD SELLING OF STOCKS—
HEAVY FALLS IN PRICES.

New York, Thursday, 24 October 1929.

A Niagara of liquidation fell upon the American Stock Exchange today. For three hours trading was completely demoralized with blocks of 10,000, 15,000 and 20,000 shares of stock pressing for sale and prices melting away 5 and 10 points at a time. Never before, even at the outbreak of the Great War, was there such a volume of transactions. Outright panic was never very far from the markets during the day until after the bankers' statement was broadcast [to the effect that trouble was technical, not fundamental].

New York, Friday, October 25th.

The Stock Markets regained their equipoise today. There was none of the panicky scenes of yesterday in Wall Street . . . and prices were steady. . . .

The public generally is apparently satisfied that there is nothing fundamentally wrong with trade and industry and is disposed to accept the idea that the crash yesterday was due chiefly to technical reasons.

New York, Monday, October 28th.

New Wall Street Collapse.

Liquidation persistent and uninterrupted overwhelmed the Stock Exchanges again today, bringing losses even greater than those sustained in the panicky market of last Thursday.

. . . The concensus of opinion at a bankers' conference held today at Messrs. Morgans' was that the worst is over in the stock market, and that the situation has taken 'an appreciable turn for the better'.

New York, Tuesday, October 29th.

There has never been such a day of liquidation on the Stock Markets as this. For the third time in less than a week stocks, good, bad and indifferent were thrown upon the market in huge blocks for what they would bring. Prices broke far below the previous low levels of the year, wiping out all gains of more than 12 months and establishing almost incredibly low levels.

By the time the market closed at 3 o'clock, the volume (of sale) was close to 17,000,000 shares, with the recording ticker more than 89 minutes behind the transactions on the floor of the New York Stock Exchange.

Even last night, before the great additional fall of today, it was reckoned that 12 stocks alone had suffered a decline in market value from their high point of this year, of 8,750,000,000 dollars (£1,750,000,000).

54. The League of Nations and the Abyssinian Crisis, 1936

(a) This general report of the Oil Committee was issued on 12 February 1936: Its main conclusions were as follows.

Source: *Keesing's Contemporary Archives*, pp. 1985-9.

1. In the conditions prevailing at the moment, the period which would have to elapse before an oil embargo, universally applied, would become fully effective, may be taken to be about three to three and a half months.

2. Such an embargo, applied by all States Members of the Co-ordination Committee—the big Sanctions Committee composed of all members of the League save Italy and Abyssinia—would be effective were the U.S.A. to limit her exports to Italy at the normal level prior to 1935.

3. If such an embargo were applied by the States Members of the Co-ordination Committee alone, the only

effect it would have on Italy would be to render her purchase of petroleum more difficult and expensive.

*   *   *

7. As regards transport, the Committee thinks that, if Italian oil had to be drawn from ports in the Gulf of Mexico, the Italian fleet might be expected to carry not less than half of Italy's consumption in 1935 (possibly as much as two million tons). The present consumption is estimated at the rate of about three and a half million tons per annum.

Italy would therefore require, in the view of the experts somewhat over 225,000 tons gross of foreign shipping for her transport services. If the embargo on transport were to be imposed by the League, there would remain for this purpose vessels belonging to the tanker fleets of the U.S.A. and Germany (between 300,000–500,000 tons, and 90,000 tons respectively).

(b) Mr. Anthony Eden's speech in the Commons, 18 July, announcing the Government's abandonment of sanctions:

Source: op. cit., p. 2153A.

*   *   *

Whatever view we take of the course of action which the League should follow, here is one fact upon which we must all be agreed. We have to admit that the purpose for which sanctions were imposed has not been realised. The Italian military campaign succeeded. That is a situation which has got to be faced. It is a situation which nothing but military action from outside the country can reverse.

Taking all these facts into consideration, His Majesty's Government have come to the conclusion that there is no longer any utility in continuing sanctions as a means of pressure upon Italy. We have got to comprise within one organisation the willing collaboration of governments of totally divergent character. I say this to give some indication of the nature of the problem, and unless we do face it, we cannot expect the League in the future effectively to meet these problems.

*　　*　　*